Modular Instruction

THE BURGESS EDUCATIONAL PSYCHOLOGY SERIES FOR THE TEACHER
Consulting Editor: John F. Feldhusen, Purdue University

Modular Instruction

A Guide to the Design, Selection, Utilization and Evaluation of Modular Materials

James D. Russell

Foreword by S. N. Postlethwait, *Purdue University*

BURGESS PUBLISHING COMPANY • MINNEAPOLIS, MINNESOTA

Foreword

This foreword is written with mixed feelings. My concern is not for the philosophy on which the content is based but relates to the further propagation of the term "module." This generic term applies to units that comprise a larger entity and is used extensively outside the field of education, e.g., components of a TV set, construction units of a building, parts of a spacecraft, and many other commonplace items outside the field of education. Even within education there is no uniformity of its use. The term is applied with various meanings such as media units of an instructional program (movie, pamphlet, videotape, audio-tape or any other component of the program), a time block of instruction, publications covering a series of related topics, short lessons, a large collection of instructional units, etc. My own bias is that education needs a term for a unit of subject matter relating specifically to content. Instructional strategy, time elements, study programs, and media components are secondary considerations and relate to the acquisition of knowledge rather than a unit of knowledge itself.

The common term, course, has been used for many years to designate units of subject matter. We have referred to courses in botany, zoology, agronomy, pharmacy, English, etc., and to all of us this term is recognized as a functional unit of education. A course requires no definition of instructional strategy, time limits or other restrictions, yet it communicates to all of us a unit of knowledge. Because the course as a unit of knowledge is large and vague, the present and future generations need a new unit or subdivision of subject matter to provide greater flexibility and adaptation to individual requirements for content, instructional strategy, study habits, and credit assignment. The obvious need is to increase the "resolving power" of the present educational unit through the use of smaller units or small courses. The concept of such a unit need not change from the present functional unit (course) but should be reduced in size to accommodate current needs. A "little course" might well be called a name consistent with our current concept of units of knowledge. In 1968 I suggested the term "microcourse," but several colleagues convinced me that a better term would be "minicourse." This term requires no overhaul in our concept of a unit of knowledge and is not encumbered by concepts derived from its use in a variety of other contexts. It does not imply, as does "module," that it is necessarily a component of some larger entity. Yet, just as courses can be variously grouped into specialities such as home economics, veterinary science and psychology, minicourses can be grouped for credit of amounts compatible with conventional units of course hours.

Aside from this feature, I feel this book can make a substantial contribution to teachers who would like to learn how to produce instructional materials in the unitized format. The author has been exposed to many practical lessons and experiences through his association with the Minicourse Development Project and workshops on the audio-tutorial approach, and he has drawn freely from these in the formulation of the content. This background coupled with his previous training at Indiana University has enabled Dr. Russell to describe the philosophy and procedures of several projects and compile this information into one "module."

October 29, 1973 S. N. Postlethwait

Preface

Even though teachers have long recognized and acknowledged individual differences in students, every member of a class is usually locked into the same instructional sequence with the same learning materials. All students are expected to learn the same content in the same amount of time. One possible solution to this problem is individualized instruction. One type of individualized instruction is modular instruction.

This book is designed to serve as a basic introduction to the concept of modular instruction. It is written for a classroom teacher. The only prerequisite is a desire to improve student learning. Examples are drawn from various disciplines and include a range of ages and grade levels. This book is the first of its kind in the area of modular instruction. In addition to including a description of what has been done in the field, it is a practical "how-to-do-it" manual for the teacher who is genuinely interested in implementing modular instruction with his students.

Modular Instruction can serve as the text for a short-course or workshop. It can serve as an adjunct text in an educational methods course, or it can be used by a teacher who wants to develop competency in the design, development and utilization of modular materials.

The chapters in this text have undergone extensive tryout and testing with hundreds of pre-service and in-service teachers. The materials have been revised on the basis of the teachers' comments, suggestions and performances on written tests as well as on their demonstrated ability to design modules. The materials have been used by student-teachers in an introductory media course, students in educational psychology courses, junior college teachers in summer institutes, in-service teachers during instructional development workshops, and teaching assistants in a college psychology course. Data has been collected from over 500 students and teachers who have used the material as a manual for designing and using modules.

As with any learning strategy, the results have been of varying success, but most instructors who have used the materials in teacher-training classes and institutes have commented that this approach was more successful than what they had tried previously. Teachers who have used the material during its development have demonstrated that they can develop effective modules for use with their students after studying and applying the techniques described herein. Teachers in courses and workshops have been given summative tests covering the objectives at the beginning of each chapter and have approached the 90/90 criterion (that is, 90 percent of the teachers mastering ninety percent or more of the objectives).

I wish to publicly express my sincere thanks to the hundreds of students—too many to list individually—who have read and studied the previous versions of this text. Their frank comments and positive suggestions were most valuable in rewriting the text to improve its effectiveness. A good formula or a good recipe means very little unless it has been tried, tested and proven. The results of these endeavors determine the true merit of any formula, recipe, or book, such as *Modular Instruction*.

I also wish to thank Joyce Andrew, Ken Bush, Deirdre Darst, Dave McGaw, Carolyn Platt, Jackie Wright, Curt Smiley, and Jo Meyer, who graciously allowed me to use their modules as examples within the text, and Joyce Bell, who patiently typed and retyped the manuscript.

A special acknowledgement goes to S. N. Postlethwait, who not only wrote the Foreword but who introduced me to modular instruction. I am pleased to be his student, friend and colleague.

Without the assistance and encouragement from John Feldhusen, editor of the *Burgess Educational Psychology Series for the Teacher*, this text would never have become a reality. His contributions and editorial assistance were most valuable in putting my thoughts and ideas together in a readable and understandable format.

Last, and by no means least, I must express my special thanks and love to my resident editor and wife Nancy, who made John Feldhusen's job much easier by modifying many sentences, paragraphs and ideas before he ever saw them. My daughter Jennifer was most understanding when I had to spend time with the typewriter instead of her.

November, 1973   James D. Russell

Contents

Goals or General Objectives,   xiii

Chapter I   Introduction to Modular Instruction,   1

Chapter II   Fundamentals of Modular Instruction,   13

Chapter III   Selection of Modules,   31

Chapter IV   Designing Modules: An Overview,   39

Chapter V   Exact Specification of Objectives,   45

Chapter VI   Construction of Criterion Items,   53

Chapter VII   Analysis of Learner Characteristics and Specification of Entry Behavior,   63

Chapter VIII   Sequencing of Instruction and Selection of Media,   69

Chapter IX   Student Tryout of the Module,   79

Chapter X   Evaluation of the Module,   87

Chapter XI   The Utilization of Modules,   95

Chapter XII   Implementing Modular Instruction,   129

References,   137

Index,   139

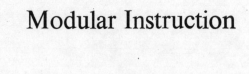

Modular Instruction

Goals or
General Objectives

After studying this text, you should be able to:
1. Identify the need for individualized instruction and describe how modular instruction can be used as one strategy to meet this need.
2. State the learning principles which underlie modular instruction.
3. List the advantages and disadvantages of modular instruction.
4. Identify the components of a module.
5. Synthesize an instructional development strategy which you can use to design modules for use in your classroom.
6. Design a multi-media module which includes a set of specific objectives, a posttest, and a description of the learner characteristics and entry behavior of the intended population.
7. Discuss and justify the fundamentals of modular instruction.
8. Develop an approach which will allow you to convert existing instructional materials into a modular format.
9. Describe the five steps in the selection process and be able to use the procedure in the selection of actual modular materials for classroom use.
10. Given a checklist (similar to the one presented in the text), evaluate a particular unit of modular instruction.
11. Describe how modules may be used in the following instructional situations: regular instruction, enrichment, remedial work, establishing entry behavior, absentee instruction and correspondence courses.
12. Synthesize a philosophy of grading which is appropriate for modular instruction.

13. Analyze various strategies for implementing modular instruction and adopt or synthesize one which you could use in your classes.
14. Discuss the types of equipment and facilities which are necessary to utilize modular instruction.
15. Implement an evaluation procedure for determining the effectiveness and efficiency of a set of given modular materials.

Introduction to Modular Instruction

After reading and studying this chapter, you should be able to:

1. *Synthesize your own definition of individualized instruction. It should be consistent with the discussion in the text.*
2. *Discuss the rationale for using modules. Your discussion should include at least five reasons.*
3. *Define "module" on the basis of the discussion and example presented in Chapter I. Acceptable performance will include a fifty word definition with five relevant characteristics included.*

Educators have talked about "individual differences" for many years.[1] A major contemporary goal of education is to provide an equal educational opportunity for students of every background, regardless of their aptitude, intelligence or previous achievement. Individualized instruction is an attempt to provide the optimum learning conditions for each individual student.

By individualized instruction is meant whatever arrangements make it possible for each student to be engaged at all times in learning those things that are of most value to himself, as an individual.[2]

Because of the restraints put upon time, money and instructional resources,

[1] John Dewey, *Democracy and Education* (New York: Macmillan Company, 1916).
[2] Thorwald Esbensen, *Independent Study in Science* (Washington, D.C.: National Science Teachers Association, 1970).

the ideal—a totally individualized instructional system—may never be reached. Even if a teacher had only one student, he could not provide totally individualized instruction as defined above because of his own inability to identify all of the student's individual needs and to make the appropriate provisions for them. However, individualized instruction can serve as a goal to work toward.

During the last two decades, a number of educational innovations have been attempted to meet the individual needs of students. Many of those innovations have already undergone much evaluation and appear to be educationally sound. Perhaps the "lockstep" curriculum and "egg crate" classroom will soon be broken, and new methods of teaching and learning will be implemented.

One of the first attempts to meet individual needs was programmed instruction. Most of the early paper-and-pencil programs were designed to teach small units of subject matter. The research of B. F. Skinner at Harvard University in the middle and late 1950's and others during this period led to the formulation of several teaching principles which became characteristic of programmed instruction—small steps, active student involvement, immediate confirmation or reinforcement and self-pacing.

In 1961, S. N. Postlethwait began using audio-taped presentations to supplement the instruction in his freshman botany course at Purdue University. During the next decade, he developed the audio-tutorial approach which is structured around a self-instructional learning carrel. The system he developed incorporated objectives, an audio tape, printed study guides, visual aids, and actual biological materials. As used in his courses, the system also provides for teaching assistants who can aid students in understanding complex concepts. The A-T approach has proven to be a very effective and successful learning experience incorporating self-pacing and multi-media materials.

The concept of a small unit of subject matter which could be treated coherently as an individual topic and could be conveniently integrated into a study program was proposed by Postlethwait in 1968.[3] He originally called these units "microcourses" but later adopted the term "minicourses" since the units were, in fact, small courses. A conventional course could be constructed from a number of microcourses or minicourses. The length and content of the small courses were determined by the objectives.

Minicourses were first implemented at Purdue University in 1969. Since then, the concept has spread to other colleges and universities as well as to both elementary and secondary schools. Just as programmed instruction emerged in the fifties and the audio-tutorial approach developed in the sixties, the thrust of the seventies is the design, development and utilization of minicourses. Purdue University has received a four-year grant from the National Science Foundation to produce minicourses for a core program in undergraduate biology.

[3] S. N. Postlethwait, "Time for Microcourses?" *The Library-College Journal*, Vol. 2, No. 2 (Winter, 1969).

Similar small units of instruction are being developed elsewhere under titles such as "concept-o-pac," "instruc-o-pac," "unipak," "learning activity package" (LAP) and "individualized learning package" (ILP), just to mention a few. The generic term which seems to be emerging in the literature is "module," hence the title of this book—*Modular Instruction*.

A module is an instructional package dealing with a single conceptual unit of subject matter. It is an attempt to individualize learning by enabling the student to master one unit of content before moving to another. The multi-media learning experiences are often presented in a self-instructional format. The student controls the rate and intensity of his study. Since the module package may involve materials which are portable, the student can take it to the library, to a study carrel or to his home. The length of a module may vary from only a few minutes of student time to several hours. The modules can be used individually or combined in a variety of different sequences.

A RATIONALE FOR MODULES

Modules afford the opportunity to develop, evaluate and use a variety of media to optimize instruction for students on a given topic. The approach can be carefully and deliberately sequenced, tried out with students and revised until the maximum achievement is demonstrated by the most students. Careful evaluation makes it possible to measure and predict the effectiveness of each module.

A wide variety of media and activities can be incorporated into modules. Examples include:

1. Reading textbooks and articles
2. Examining diagrams and photographs
3. Viewing films and colored slides
4. Handling real objects and models
5. Studying demonstration materials
6. Listening to audio tapes
7. Conducting actual or simulated experiments
8. Discussing subject matter with other students and teachers.

All sensory inputs can and should be available to the students to meet the objectives of the module. Each student can use any or all of the media and materials available. The selection of the most appropriate approach is often left to the student.

Individualized

Depending upon how they are used, modules can be highly individualized, or they can provide uniform instruction for a large number of students on an individual basis. Alternative modules can present different content or different approaches to the same content. Alternatives allow each student to select the module most appropriate for him and to study at a pace and a time most convenient and effective for him. He can pace his study according to his own ability to assimilate the information and master the objectives. Exposure to difficult subject matter can be repeated as often as necessary. Thus, all students can master the material, and the slower ones are not forced to move on prematurely to new material.

Flexible

Flexibility for both the student and the teacher is another characteristic of modules. The small units of subject matter can be arranged or sequenced in a variety of formats. One module might meet part of the requirements for several regular courses. The student might have the option of completing any ten of a total of fifteen or twenty modules to meet the requirements of a "total course." The student might also be free to select the order in which he studies some of the modules.

Freedom

Modules can provide a maximum of student freedom for independent study. Modules also place the responsibility for learning squarely on the shoulders of the student. The emphasis is on student learning rather than on the teacher's teaching. The activities of the student are directed, not the activities of the teacher. A disadvantage of modules can be a lack of interest on the part of the students. Since the teacher is not always present and watching over his shoulder, the student may not be motivated, or forced in some cases, to pursue the learning activity. Therefore, it is still necessary for the module and the teacher to create an environment in which the learner is inspired to become involved in the process of learning.

Active Participation

One of the most important features which should be incorporated into modules is the opportunity for active student participation. It has long been known that students learn by doing.[4] Therefore, modules should always provide for active involvement, thus replacing the more passive reading of the text or just listening to the teacher with handling learning materials, manipulating equipment and responding frequently to pertinent questions.

Since modules are in an individual, self-instructional format, make-up lessons and review sessions are accomplished with a minimum of effort. Modules give each student the advantage of individualized instruction and at the same time provide for effective learning by large numbers of students. Uniform but

---

[4] Jerome S. Bruner, *Toward a Theory of Instruction* (Cambridge, Mass.: Harvard University Press, 1966).

independent instruction allows every student to progress at his own rate whether he is a member of a class of twenty or two hundred. All students can be exposed to the same material, regardless of the hour of the day or the day of the week.

Teacher's Role

Some critics feel that modules are devoid of human interaction. The criticism is valid if the teacher uses modules as an excuse to spend class time in the teacher's lounge or his office. The teacher should be available to answer students' questions and to provide encouragement if needed. When modules are used, the teacher is freed from the routine and repetitive activities of teaching the same material again and again.

For example, in foreign language instruction the teacher no longer has to be in charge of drill and vocabulary building activities. The teacher need not hold the flashcards or repeat the new words for the lesson. A module can be designed to present the printed words with an audiotape to accurately provide the correct pronunciation again and again. Once the module has been developed, the teacher is available to devote more time to the important activities of teaching—inspiration, motivation, orientation and personal contact. The teacher's role becomes one of diagnostician, prescriber and resource person.

Student Interaction

Modules can be designed to provide student-to-student interaction. Students should be encouraged to work together on complex learning activities. They can discuss difficult subject matter areas and quiz each other on the topic. Many students find it helpful to tutor each other and assist one another in developing mastery of the materials.

Modules can be open-ended, thus allowing the student to determine the direction in which he wishes to proceed with the topic after he has mastered the basic subject matter. The additional study may be selected from a variety of activities, sometimes called "quests," or the study may be original, that is, designed by the student himself.

Rather than trying to define module, let's look at parts of an actual module. This particular module was designed for students in biology at either the high school or introductory college level.

EXCERPTS FROM A MINICOURSE ON "MIMICRY"[5]

Try to imagine yourself as a student participating in a "minicourse" (the specific type of module being developed at Purdue University). As you read the

[5] "Mimicry" was designed and developed by Deirdre S. Darst under National Science Foundation grant #GY 7664 to the Minicourse Development Project at Purdue University. Copyright © 1971, Purdue Research Foundation.

FIGURE A
Student seated at carrel working through minicourse on "Mimicry." Note
real specimens mounted in display case, audiotape player, slide projector
and study guide.

transcribed audio script, view the study guide reproduced and see the real
specimens pictured, you must realize that the printed format is a poor substitute
for the real sights and sounds that make up the actual learning experience.
However, this excerpt should give you an introduction to the concept of
modular instruction and its potential.

(Page from Mimicry *Study Guide)*

Abstract

This minicourse is a brief descriptive approach to mimicry. The classic case of the Viceroy and Monarch butterflies is discussed including a short discussion of the role of natural selection in the evolution of the mimic type. Mention is made of the work of Brower to show experimental evidence of mimicry. Many examples are described; insects mimicking other insects, insects mimicking plants and plants resembling insects. Olfactory mimicry in the cuckoo-pint is discussed together with its relationship to pollination. Insectivorous plants are introduced including the pitcher plant which mimics a flower and a type of venus fly trap whose leaves resemble flowers. Accoustical mimicry in birds is mentioned briefly. The parasitic habit of the European cuckoo is included with a discussion of the mimic nature of her egg color and pattern when compared with the host egg. In conclusion, the angling turtle and the angler fish are included to show how they display dummy bait in order to lure in their prey.

Objectives

Upon completing this minicourse, the student will:

1. give an example of a hymenopteran model and a dipteran mimic and describe the type of protection received by the impostor. Mention should be made of the protective characteristic possessed by hymenopterans and a structural characteristic by which one might tell the difference between a wasp and a fly.
2. explain how the pattern of the mimic Viceroy butterfly came about in terms of natural selection. The explanation must include mention of how the first appearance of the mimic might have occurred and of the ensuing gradual change in the gene pool.
3. design an experiment to demonstrate that living things can enjoy protection from predators by the employment of mimicry. The experiment must include a predator-prey relationship, a model and mimic relationship and a control.
4. give an example of any two of the following: a plant which mimics an insect, a plant which employs olfactory mimicry or plant leaves which mimic a flower. For each plant selected, the student will describe the benefit received by the plant and how this benefit relates to survival.

You enter the learning center and sit down at a booth. Before you are all the information and materials which you will need to master the concept of "mimicry." (See Figure A.) You skim the abstract to get an overview of what is contained in the minicourse; then you carefully read the objectives to learn exactly what will be expected of you upon completing the minicourse.

Now position your headphones, start the tape player and hear:

Today we will be looking at the clever phenomenon of mimicry in nature. To help you get an idea of what we'll be talking about, take a look at the two

FIGURE B
Butterflies 1a and 1b in the "Mimicry" display case.

butterflies labelled 1a and 1b in the case. (See Figure B.) *Do you think they are the same species?* Pause. *Actually they are of two completely different species. Suppose now that you are walking through a meadow and you spot one of these butterflies flitting from flower to flower. Could you say for sure which butterfly you had seen? Probably not. Let's look together a little more closely at these two butterflies. Perhaps we can find some points which might distinguish one from the other. The one tagged 1a is the Monarch butterfly. You may already be familiar with this insect since it is renowned for its lengthy migrations. The other butterfly, 1b, is the Viceroy butterfly. Can you see any differences by which you might tell them apart?* Pause. *We might say the Monarch is a little larger than the Viceroy or note that the abdomen is longer on the Monarch, but these are rather vague distinguishing points. The only sure way I can tell if I see one of these elusive creatures is to look for a black line running parallel to the edges of the hind wings. You can see this in the Viceroy. Notice that this line is absent in the Monarch.*

The Monarch is apparently very nasty tasting to birds. Thus, birds will avoid it when seeking food if they have already experienced the taste of the insect. However, the other butterfly, the Viceroy, would make a very tasty meal for any bird who cared to try it. Being tasty is definitely a disadvantage but what advantage do you suppose the Viceroy has by looking like the Monarch? Turn to page 1 in your study guide and write down your ideas. Turn off the tape while you do this.

In Exercise I, the student is using a multi-sensory approach to learning. He has the real specimens before him, hears a description of the butterflies and is then asked to make observations before actively responding in the study guide. Upon returning to the tape, he is reinforced with the correct answers.

(Page 1 from Mimicry *Study Guide)*

Part 1. Viceroy or Monarch???

Exercise I

List any advantages and disadvantages you can think of in being a Viceroy butterfly.

Advantages   *Disadvantages*

A. The distasteful Monarch is termed the model organism and the similarly patterned but tasty Viceroy is called the mimic.

B. In the late 1800's an English naturalist, Henry Bates, described the phenomenon of mimicry and it was given the name Batesian mimicry in his honor.

What did you come up with? Perhaps you decided that the Viceroy reminded the birds of the Monarch and you are so right. Then it should follow that upon recognizing the Monarch butterfly, a bird will avoid using it as food. Since the Viceroy looks so much like the nasty tasting Monarch it seems logical that it should enjoy the same protection from being eaten by a bird even though it is quite tasty. The Monarch is then termed the model organism, and the Viceroy is the mimic.

(Page 2 from Mimicry *Study Guide)*

Part 2. *Experimental Evidence of Mimicry*

Exercise II

An experiment to show the evidence of mimicry.

Materials

Starlings
Mealworms
Orange cellulose paint
Green cellulose paint
Quinine dihydrochloride (this is a very bitter substance)

Question

Given the materials above, how could you attempt to show that a mimic would be avoided as prey? See how you manage with this and then turn the page to check your work.

This idea of mimicry surfaced during the latter half of the 1800's when the English naturalist Henry Bates was wandering through the forests of Brazil. He collected ninety-four butterfly species which he first classified as all belonging to the same family. Today, only twenty-seven of the original ninety-four are still left in this family. The remaining sixty-seven have been placed in a completely different family. Bates noted that some distasteful animals possess such a conspicuous color or pattern that they are recognized by prospective enemies. This type of conspicuous coloration is known as warning coloration. A good example of warning coloration is possessed by skunks with their conspicuous black and white bands. Bates further noted that once a predator has sampled a nasty tasting prey, it would be unlikely that it would be sampled a second time if it had a conspicuous enough warning pattern. Thus, he decided that it should be possible for an edible organism which resembles a distasteful organism to enjoy the same protection from enemies. Such animals are said to possess a false

(Page 3 from **Mimicry** *Study Guide)*

Part 2 *(Continued)*

The Important Components of Exercise II

Starlings—Predators

Mealworms—Prey

Orange paint—Control

Green paint—Coloration of the model and the mimic

Quinine dihydrochloride—For making the model unpalatable (Of course, it makes no difference to which part of the experiment you assigned the colors.)

An Experiment Performed by Brower (1960) Using the Above Materials

Brower fed starlings with normal mealworms, two segments of which were painted orange. Other mealworms were made distasteful and painted green on the same segments. A third category included normal untreated mealworms with the same two segments painted green. There is no evidence in nature that green functions as a warning color and that orange is harmless. Thus, the possibility of any innate reaction entering the experiment was avoided.

Here are some results Brower obtained from the experiment.

1. The starlings soon learned to avoid all green colored mealworms whether they were distasteful or not.
2. The green banded category of mealworms was avoided even when 60% edible and 40% distasteful were presented to the birds. This means that the number of mimics can exceed the number of models and still receive protection.
3. The starlings ate all the orange banded mealworms.
4. If a bird erred and picked up a model by mistake it was spat out immediately.

---

warning pattern; they "act a part." An actor performs a mime and so the presentation of a false warning pattern was named mimicry. Since Bates was the first to point out the phenomenon, it is given the name "Batesian mimicry" in his honor.

Has it been proved that mimics do receive protection similar to that received by the models? There are some experiments that have been designed and clearly demonstrate that birds avoid offensive organisms as prey and also the palatable mimics. Now, I'd like you to try your hand at designing an experiment to show this. You'll find the components of the experiment on page 2 of your study guide. Turn off the tape while you do this.

After the student turns to page 2 of the study guide, he designs his own experiment to demonstrate the concept of mimicry. From the information given, the student is able to become actively involved and to synthesize an experiment. He then returns to the tape for a discussion of the experiment by the teacher.

How did you do? Did you paint your model worms and your mimic worms the same color, the only difference being that you made your models taste bitter? Did you use the other color of paint to make control mealworms? If you did, then your experiment should look something like the one performed by Brower, described on page 3 of your study guide.

After turning to page 3 of the study guide, the student is presented with an experiment actually conducted by Brower. The student can compare his design with that of Brower. He is then ready to return to the tape and complete the module.

Summary

Modules are a recent attempt to individualize instruction. They provide a variety of learning strategies and a wide selection of media. Their prime attribute is that they provide a systematized way of developing and implementing subject matter content and processes. A systematic approach for developing modules will be described in detail in Chapters IV through X.

In addition to providing a form of individualized instruction, modules allow for flexibility in the selection and utilization of instructional materials. Closely associated with this flexibility is freedom for both the student and the teacher. The student is free to study at his own pace, and the teacher is freed from repetitious presentation of information.

Most importantly, the student is actively involved in learning. No longer does he take a passive role of just reading and listening; instead, he is actively involved in responding to instructional materials, manipulating media and equipment, as well as interacting with other students and the instructor.

Goldschmid and Goldschmid[6] defined module as:

A self-contained, independent unit of a planned series of learning activities designed to help the student accomplish certain well-defined objectives.

Chapter II describes the basic attributes of modules. Even though we have defined "module" and presented an example in this chapter, it is important to look at the fundamental characteristics of modules in order to understand their full potential.

[6]Barbara Goldschmid and Marcel L. Goldschmid, "Modular Instruction: Principles and Applications in Higher Education," *Learning and Development*, Vol. 3, No. 8 (April/May 1972).

Fundamentals of Modular Instruction

After reading and studying this chapter, you should be able to:

1. *Discuss at least seven characteristics of modular instruction. Your discussion should include approximately a one-hundred word explanation of each characteristic.*
2. *Compare modular instruction with conventional instruction. Acceptable performance will include comparing the two on at least ten attributes of instruction.*

Having looked at excerpts of a sample module, let's examine some of the fundamental characteristics of modular instruction. Any given module may *not* have all of the characteristics, but these are the general characteristics of modular instruction:

1. Self-contained, self-instructional package
2. Concern for individual differences
3. Statement of objectives
4. Association, structure and sequence of knowledge
5. Utilization of a variety of media
6. Active participation by the learner
7. Immediate reinforcement of responses
8. Mastery evaluation strategy

13

SELF-CONTAINED, SELF-INSTRUCTIONAL PACKAGE

The modular concept utilizes a self-contained instructional package pertaining to a single concept or unit of subject matter. The approach is a multi-sensory learning experience which actively involves the student. The student is given the opportunity to conduct a self-paced study with "instant replay" characteristics. Furthermore, modules can be sequenced in a variety of patterns to build a unique course of study for students with different interests and needs.

A basic assumption made in the development of modules is that learning is a process which must be done by the learner.[1] This underlying assumption has important implications with respect to the subject matter arrangement, the types of media employed and the allowances made for individual differences in the learners. This assumption can be regarded as the basic rationale underlying modular instruction, and it determines the educational principles used. The principles of learning employed in the modular format are principles derived from learning theory that can be applied to a wide variety of learning conditions.[2]

In the case of the module on mimicry, all the materials fit into a carton measuring twelve inches by ten inches by eight inches. The self-contained package is lightweight and could be easily carried from the learning center to the student's home. All the materials would be available for the student on a self-instructional basis. The nature of the subject (mimicry) lends itself to a number of applications (such as high school biology, general science) or just to student interest and enjoyment. Since the entire module only requires about an hour of student time, it could be sequenced easily into a variety of learning programs.

CONCERN FOR INDIVIDUAL DIFFERENCES

In a "normal" class, there are many individual differences among the learners. It is usually impossible for the teacher to simultaneously meet all the needs of each individual pupil, so he must follow a course which will present the least difficulty for the greatest number of pupils. The results of this compromise are that some students may find the pace of the lesson too fast and others may find that the lesson proceeds too slowly. Some of the individual differences which may be cited as significant for the learning process are: differences in intellectual ability, differences in academic background and differences in the manner of

---

[1] S. N. Postlethwait, J. Novak, and H. T. Murray, *The Audio-Tutorial Approach to Learning* (Minneapolis: Burgess Publishing, 1972).

[2] Boree, M. Ray, *Educational Psychology* (New York: The Ronald Press, 1959).

learning—some students learn more quickly by aural methods and others learn more quickly by visual methods.

Self-instructional modules allow the rate of learning to be adjusted to suit the needs of each individual student. The slow learner is able to repeat any part of the program which he found difficult, and the fast learner is able to move quickly through the program if he can satisfy the objectives which have been set for that module. In many modules students work alone, thus allowing for individual differences in learning rates. A number of studies have been undertaken to find the optimum group size for maximum learning, but the results have been inconclusive. Sutter and Reid[3] carried out an experiment at the University of Texas in which one hundred male students were divided into two groups. One group of students worked alone, and the other group of students worked in pairs. The students were all given tests prior to the experiment to determine their level of achievement, sociability and test anxiety. It was found that when the level of achievement was controlled the students high in sociability and low in test anxiety achieved better in pairs, but those low in sociability and high in test anxiety achieved better alone (see also footnote 4).

Research may be able to show that for some students there is an advantage in working in pairs or small groups. If so, the module could be adapted or designed to make provision for more than one student. In the meantime with the present state of research in this field, the methods used in modular instruction often combine individual study with small group work. The student has the advantage of self-pacing, and, at the same time, he is able to benefit from the interaction with other students and the teacher.

The possibility of accommodating individual differences is one of the most important characteristics of modules. In the "Mimicry" module, the student has control of the pace of the lesson since he can start, stop and reverse the audio tape. He can listen to parts of the tape as often as necessary to learn the material. The same information is often presented in both the audio and visual mode, as in the case of the experimental design for Exercise II.

STATEMENT OF OBJECTIVES

Clearly stated objectives perform a useful function for the developer of the instructional materials, the teacher and the student in directing the teaching/learning process. At the developmental level, the objectives give

---

[3] E. G. Sutter and B. Reid, "Learner Variables and Interpersonal Conditions in Computer Assisted Instruction," *Journal of Educational Psychology*, 60 (3, 1969): 153-57.

[4] James Hartley, "Some Factors Affecting Student Performance in Programmed Learning," *Programmed Learning and Educational Technology*, 5(July, 1963): 3.

direction and focus; the developer knows where he is going before he begins designing instructional activities so that each medium and activity is aimed at meeting a specific objective. For the teacher, objectives give insight into the content and the appropriateness of the module for his students. For the student, they describe exactly what is expected of him and provide him with a goal to be mastered. Hence, the student's learning activities become goal-oriented. Modules take full advantage of the benefits of a clear statement of objectives.

Considerable research has been undertaken in recent years on educational and instructional objectives. A summary of this research is provided by Edling.[5] Much of the research which has been carried out has been stimulated by the increasing amount of instructional media available. The use of instructional objectives has grown primarily out of the process of task analysis in business and military settings. The insistence on the importance of specifying educational objectives in terms of observable behavior has been one outstanding contribution of programmed instruction to education. In a programmed booklet originally titled *Preparing Objectives for Programmed Instruction*[6], Robert Mager characterizes objectives in the following way:

1. A statement of instructional objectives is a collection of words or symbols describing one of your educational *intents*.
2. An objective will communicate your intent to the degree that you have *described* what the learner will be doing when demonstrating his achievement and how you will know when he is doing it.
3. To describe terminal behavior . . .
   a. Identify and name the over-all behavior act.
   b. Define the important conditions under which the behavior is to occur.
   c. Define the criterion of acceptable performance.

As was done in the module on mimicry, the student beginning a module is usually requested to read the objectives as a first step before going ahead with the unit of study.

Objectives are also helpful in constructing test items. Once the objectives have been written, it is a relatively simple matter to convert the objective into a test item. Here are some examples from the "Mimicry" minicourse:

Objective A

The student will give an example of a hymenopteran model and a dipteran mimic and describe the type of protection received by the impostor. Mention

---

[5] Jack V. Edling, "Educational Media," *Review of Educational Research, 38(2):* Chapter 4.

[6] Robert F. Mager, *Preparing Instructional Objectives* (Palo Alto, Calif.: Fearon Publishers, 1962).

should be made of the protective characteristic possessed by hymenoptera and a structural characteristic by which one might tell the difference between a wasp and a fly.

Test Item (A)

Give an example of a hymenopteran model and a dipteran mimic and describe the type of protection received by the impostor.

Objective B

The student will explain how the pattern of the mimic Viceroy butterfly came about in terms of natural selection. The explanation must include mention of how the first appearance of the mimic might have occurred and of the ensuing gradual change in the gene pool.

Test Item (B)

Explain briefly how the Viceroy butterfly came to resemble the Monarch butterfly. Give your answer in terms of natural selection.

Objective C

The student will design an experiment to demonstrate that living things can enjoy protection from predators by the employment of mimicry. The experiment must include a predator-prey relationship, a model and mimic relationship and a control.

Test Item (C)

How would you show experimental evidence of mimicry using sunflower seeds and your own choice of predator?

Objective D

The student will give an example of any two of the following: a plant which mimics an insect, a plant which employs olfactory mimicry or plant leaves which mimic flowers. For each plant selected, the student will describe the benefit received by the plant and how this benefit relates to survival.

Test Item (D)

Give an example of any two of the following: a plant which mimics an insect, a plant which employs olfactory mimicry or plant leaves which mimic flowers. For each plant selected, describe the benefit received by the plant and how this benefit relates to survival.

ASSOCIATION, STRUCTURE AND SEQUENCE OF KNOWLEDGE

The concept of "association" has been used in psychology as an explanation of how one idea begets another. In 1908, William James wrote:

> In mental terms, the more other facts a fact is associated with in the mind, the better possession of it our memory retains. Each of its associates becomes a hook to which it hangs, a means to fish it up by when sunk beneath the surface. Together they form a network of attachments by which it is woven into the entire tissue of our thoughts.[7]

Modules permit the association in time and in space of objects and of instructional media. The student is able to examine the real object and listen to the voice of the instructor and relate both to a diagram in a textbook or study guide. Postlethwait[8] has found that a convenient arrangement of materials in a booth leads to a pleasant learning experience for the student but that students may become frustrated if the items in the booth are not spatially related.

In the construction of a module, attention is given to the most appropriate sequencing of meaningful material. Basic ideas upon which subsequent information is dependent are presented first. The importance attached to the structure and the sequencing of learning events in modules is aligned with the views of leading educational theorists. Gagné[9] considers that a program of instruction should be sequenced on a hierarchy of knowledge, each terminal objective in the program requiring its own hierarchy. Gagné would make allowance for individual differences in learner background by letting each individual start the program at an appropriate point in the hierarchy. In contrast to Gagné, Mager[10] holds that the learning sequence which is most meaningful to the instructor is unlikely to be the learning sequence most meaningful to the student. Mager proposes that individual differences can be overcome by allowing the learner to generate his own learning sequence thus relating what he needs to know with what he already knows. If the sequence of learning events does not suit a student, then with appropriately designed modular instruction he is free to alter the sequence to suit his own particular needs.

The association of learning materials in "Mimicry" is described by the real objects, the study guide and the instructor's voice on the audio tape. With the objectives as a goal, the student is free to structure the learning activities in any manner he pleases; the audio tape serves only as a guide. The final sequence of information and activities as presented in a module, such as "Mimicry," is deter-

---

[7] W. James, *Psychology* (New York: Holt, 1908), p. 294.

[8] Postlethwait, et al., *The Audio-Tutorial Approach to Learning.*

[9] Robert M. Gagné, "The Acquisition of Knowledge," *Psychological Review,* 69 (1962): 355-65.

[10] Robert F. Mager, "On the Sequencing of Instructional Content" in De Cecco *Educational Technology* (New York: Holt, Rinehart and Winston, 1964).

mined by trying out the material with a variety of students. It is the developer's "best guess" as to that sequence which will be most effective with the greatest number of students.

UTILIZATION OF A VARIETY OF MEDIA

Students differ in their responsiveness to different media.[11] Some learn best through reading; others learn more from pictures and films; and still others must hear in order to understand. Some students need to get their hands on the object being studied. Most benefit from human interaction and its associated reinforcement. A module on flowers would allow a student to read about flowers, to hear about flowers from an expert via audio tape, to see them, to handle them and to smell them. Modular instruction can provide an opportunity for the student to cover the subject matter—perhaps a better word would be "uncover"—in a variety of ways and to allow each student to select the medium through which he is reached most directly and effectively. In fact, a combination of media is the best "mix" for most students.

All media can be classified into five categories.

1. Printed Materials

The student may be presented information via a textbook or an article. For modular units of instruction, student study guides can provide procedures, diagrams, and written instructions as illustrated by the "Mimicry" study guide reproduced in Chapter 1. The study guide or text may provide places for student response to questions similar to those used in programmed instruction.

2. Visuals and Projected Materials

Diagrams, photographs, color slides and films can greatly enhance a modular package. The student can be asked to analyze the visuals or to find information presented in charts or on graphs. Colored slides were used extensively in the module on mimicry. Short single-concept films are also useful since they can provide action when it is necessary for learning as in teaching a process or manipulative skills.

3. Audio Materials

Sound recordings can add realism to modules in addition to teaching auditory discrimination. The most obvious uses of audio materials would be with modules teaching foreign languages and music. The audio tape was used to present the

---

[11]J. R. Jenkins and J. D. Russell, "Involving Students in Individualized Instruction," *The American Biology Teacher* 33 (1971): 489-92.

sound of a cardinal and a mockingbird mimicking a cardinal in the sample module on mimicry. Audio input can also be used to describe the material being presented or to sequence the instruction as in the audio-tutorial approach. Postlethwait[12] feels that the audio should not be a "lecture on tape"; rather, it should be a medium that allows the teacher to *tutor* an individual student. Audio instructions also free the student's hands to manipulate materials as in a module on how to play the drums in which the student needs both hands to hold the sticks.

4. Tangible or Real Materials

Modular instruction can give students the opportunity to see real objects or their models, to handle real materials and to manipulate equipment. Handling a specimen, such as a frog or a piece of pottery, provides an excellent opportunity to get the student actively involved in learning. It is extremely important to use real objects whenever possible as an integral part of a module. Scale models, preserved specimens and plastic mounts should be used only when it is impractical to use the real thing. The student should be asked to make firsthand observations of the actual materials being studied.

5. Direct Human Interaction

The often forgotten medium in modular instruction is the teacher and the classmates. Modular instruction need not be dehumanized by solitude. Although the student is free to proceed at his own pace, he should be encouraged to interact with other students and the instructor. In fact, modular instruction can be programmed to provide for student-student interaction as well as student-instructor contact. This personal contact can clarify the subject matter, answer questions raised by the module and enrich the students' interests.

ACTIVE PARTICIPATION BY THE LEARNER

Most modules encourage the student to actively participate in the lesson. Since the student is usually in control of the lesson, he decides when to move ahead, when to study the specimen, when to answer the questions in the study guide and whether or not to repeat a section of the module which he has not understood well. In a large class of students, it is possible, and indeed likely, that at any given time many of the students will not be active participants. At a given moment, lecturing commands the attention of only about ten percent of the audience. The activity of the student in a module is not a guarantee that the

---

[12]Postlethwait, et al., *The Audio-Tutorial Approach to Learning.*

student will learn, but it does ensure that he is in a state of readiness in which learning is a possible outcome.

It is not unreasonable to suppose that the activity of a learner and the consequent reinforcement is directly related to the size of the class. Skinner[13] has argued,

> In a small class the precurrent behavior of listening, reading, solving problems and composing sentences is reinforcing frequently and almost immediately, but in a large lecture course the consequences are infrequent and deferred. If mediating devices are not set up, if the student is not automatically reinforced for knowing that he knows he stops working, and the aversion by-products of not knowing build up.

Modules usually reduce the size of the class to one, so that the teacher-pupil ratio is at an optimum, judged on this criterion. Theoretical considerations and experimental investigation are in agreement that it is desirable, in order for learning to proceed efficiently, that the learner must be an active participant in the lesson. Modules encourage maximum participation of the student.

For example, in the "Mimicry" module the student is asked to stop the tape and actually design an experiment to "prove" the concept of mimicry rather than just being told the design of the experiment. In other modules, the student may engage in physical activity such as constructing a picture frame with nails and boards, practicing free throws in physical education or classifying a set of buttons in elementary science. The activity in modules is based on the principle that a student learns what he does, therefore he must actively practice that which he is to learn.

IMMEDIATE REINFORCEMENT OF RESPONSES

Reinforcement refers to any of the wide variety of conditions which may be introduced into the learning situation whereby the probability of a given response occurring again in a similar situation is increased.[14] The theoretical positions taken on the way in which reinforcement operates are beyond the scope of this text, but it is sufficient to note that different points of view are adopted by different psychologists. The empirical work of Skinner has provided a foundation on which developers of programmed instruction and modules have been able to build. Skinner[15] says,

---

[13]B. F. Skinner, *The Technology of Teaching* (New York: Appleton, Century, Crofts, 1968), p. 156.

[14]J. G. Holland and B. F. Skinner, *The Analysis of Behavior* (New York: McGraw-Hill, 1961).

[15]B. F. Skinner, "Reinforcement Today," *American Psychologist,* 13(9, 1958): 94-99.

Programmed instruction is primarily a scheme for making an effective use of reinforcers, not only for shaping the kinds of behavior but of maintaining the behavior in strength. A program does not specify a particular kind of reinforcer . . . but it is designed to make weak reinforcers, or small measures of strong ones effective.

Modules, like programmed instruction units, use reinforcement of the correct response in shaping behavior, but do so without the small step size of paper-and-pencil programs. The student determines the step size. A delay in the reinforcement leads to a loss of efficiency in the desired response. In the ordinary classroom situation, there is frequently a long delay between the response and the reinforcement. The reinforcement in the case of the module can be arranged so that it is immediate.

For example, the student may be asked to provide a written response to a question or activity. When he has made the response, the correct answer or a "model" answer can be provided on the next page of the study guide (as in programmed instruction), with a two-by-two slide or by verbal reinforcement from the instructor on the audio tape in the case of audio-tutorial modules. The nature of these types of reinforcement lacks the rewards of social recognition which may be obtained in the classroom. On the other hand, the student may be more frequently rewarded than he would be in a large class. Modular instruction can also provide more freedom for the instructor to interact with students individually on a one-to-one basis.

MASTERY EVALUATION STRATEGY

Many modules are used in an evaluation system which requires mastery of the objectives to a prespecified criterion or level of performance before the student proceeds to the next module in the sequence. This minimizes failure and helps to assure that the student has an understanding of the material before moving on to the next unit. Benjamin S. Bloom[16] states,

Most students (perhaps over 90 percent) can master what we have to teach them, and it is the task of instruction to find the means which will enable our students to master the subject under consideration. Our basic task is to determine what we mean by mastery of the subject and to search for the methods and materials which will enable the largest proportion of our students to attain such mastery.

Unfortunately, many teachers have been conditioned by the "normal" curve and regard it as a "sacred cow" in education. The normal curve is designed to detect differences between students. Often the failures in a class are determined

[16] B. S. Bloom, J. T. Hastings, and G. F. Madaus, *Formative and Summative Evaluation of Student Learning* (New York: McGraw-Hill, 1971).

by the rank order of the students rather than by the students' failure to learn the essential ideas of the course. Education is a purposeful activity and should seek to have the students learn. If the instruction is effective, the distribution of achievement should be very different from the normal curve. In fact, it can be claimed that the educational effects have been unsuccessful to the extent to which the distribution of achievement approximates a normal curve.

John Carroll[17] proposed a strategy for mastery learning about ten years ago. He listed five factors affecting learning.

1. Aptitude for Particular Kinds of Learning

In Carroll's view, aptitude is a measure of the amount of time required by the student to attain mastery of a learning task. His assumption is that, given enough time, all students can conceivably attain mastery of a learning task. If Carroll is correct, then mastery learning is theoretically available to all. Aptitude is a measure of learning rate, not achievement level.

2. Quality of Instruction

Carroll defines the quality of instruction in terms of the degree to which the presentation, explanation and ordering of elements of the task to be learned approach the optimum for a given learner. The quality of instruction is to be considered in terms of its effect on individual learners rather than on a random group of students.

3. Ability to Understand Instruction

In most courses at the high school and college level, there is a single teacher and a single set of instructional materials. If the student has facility in understanding the teacher's communications about the learning and the instructional material (usually a textbook), he has little difficulty learning the subject. If he has difficulty in understanding the teacher's instruction and/or the instructional material, he is likely to have great difficulty learning the subject. The ability to understand instruction may be defined as the ability of the learner to understand the nature of the task he is to learn and the procedure he is to follow in the learning of the task.

4. Perseverance

Carroll defines perseverance as the time the learner is willing to spend in learning. If a student needs to spend a certain amount of time to master a particular task and he spends less than this amount in active learning, he is not likely to master the task. Perseverance does appear to be related to attitudes

[17]John A. Carroll, "A Model of School Learning," *Teachers College Record,* 64 (1963): 723-33.

toward and interest in learning. Students appear to approach different learning tasks with different amounts of perseverance. As a student finds the efforts rewarding, he is likely to spend more time on a particular learning task. If, on the other hand, the student is frustrated in his learning, he must (in self-defense) reduce the amount of time he devotes to learning. Although the frustration level of students may vary, all students will sooner or later give up a task if it is too painful for them.

5. Time Allowed for Learning

According to Carroll, the time spent on learning is the key to mastery. His basic assumption is that aptitude determines the rate of learning and that most, if not all, students can achieve mastery if they devote the amount of time needed to the learning. This implies that the student must not only devote the amount of time he needs to the learning task but also that he be allowed enough time for the learning to take place.

If learning materials were of perfect effectiveness, all students would master all of the objectives. The correlation of posttest scores with basic ability (aptitude) would be zero. To the extent that learning materials are not perfectly effective, the probability of a student's success increases with his score on a test of basic ability. With modular materials, it has been found that frequent feedback can reduce the time (and perseverance) required to attain mastery.

If students are to develop mastery learning, teachers must be able to recognize when students have achieved it. They must be able to define what is meant by mastery, and they must be able to collect the necessary evidence to establish whether or not a student has achieved it. The specification of the objectives and content of instruction is one necessary prerequisite for informing both teachers and students about the expectations. The translation of the specifications (objectives) into evaluation procedures (test items) helps to further define what the student should be able to do when he has completed the module.

SUMMARY

With the *modular approach*, the emphasis is not on the class as a whole but on individuals—each with different abilities and limitations. There is an attempt to analyze the abilities of each student at the beginning of instruction to find out exactly what each student can do and what he cannot do. There is a clear definition of the educational objectives; the instructor knows exactly what each student is learning and can follow his progress. The curriculum is subdivided into small, manageable units. There is a wide variety of learning materials in the classroom or learning center—audiotapes, records, programmed materials, slides, filmstrips, tangibles, etc. The progress of each student is measured, not in relation to the other students, but in relation to what the individual student is expected to learn.

Postlethwait and Russell[18] provide a comparison of conventional lessons with modular instruction. Their comparison summarizes the key points presented in this chapter.

Attribute	
Conventional Lesson	*Module*

Learning Experiences

Conventional materials are typically characterized by lectures, reading the text, group discussions and sometimes an isolated laboratory experience. The learning experiences are oriented toward teacher performance and group instruction with emphasis on teaching.	Modules provide for a combination of learning experiences providing an integrated sequence so that each learning activity can enhance and complement the others. The learning experiences are oriented toward student performance and individual instruction with emphasis on learning.

Role of Teacher

The role of the teacher is one of disseminator of information.	The role of the teacher is one of diagnostician, prescriber, motivator and resource person.

Objectives

Objectives are *not* usually stated in specific, behavioral terms. They must be inferred from the content of the subject matter and tests.	Objectives are stated in terms of student performance and usually are presented to the student before the instruction begins.

Selection

Materials (texts, etc.) are selected first; tests are designed to sample this material; but desired behavior with respect to the materials is not always clearly defined in advance.	Objectives are stated first; test items are designed to measure mastery of these objectives; then instructional materials are selected to assist the student in mastering the objectives.

[18]S. N. Postlethwait and James D. Russell, "Minicourses—The Style of the Future?" in *Modules* (Commission on Undergraduate Education in the Biological Sciences, 1971).

Conventional Lesson	*Module*

Rate

Students are forced to go through the course "in a lockstep manner" (all going at the *same* rate). They all begin at the same time and are expected to finish simultaneously.	Each student can proceed at his own rate. He is free to skip any portion of the module as long as he can demonstrate mastery of the objectives. He is also free to repeat any portion of the module as often as necessary.

Strategies

Teachers tend to use just one or two strategies, such as lectures and written assignments, regardless of the many different types of learning in the course (psychomotor manipulations, cognitive skills and attitudinal changes).	Different learning strategies are used for objectives representing different kinds of learning. A variety of instructional strategies are used to optimize learning on a given topic.

Media

Media are prepared and used on the basis of familiarity (texts, films, 2x2" slides, etc.) and are chosen by the teacher on the basis of his feeling comfortable with certain media (usually printed).	Media are selected to complement the type of objective and type of learner, then student tested. A large variety of media are incorporated into each module.

Individualization

Conventional lessons are group oriented. Students are usually provided with a limited number of instructional resources. Usually, the teacher specifies exactly how the student should proceed—read twenty pages of the text and answer ten questions, etc.	Modules may be highly individualized. Each student can use any or all of the media and materials available. The selection of the most appropriate approach is often left to the student—listen to a tape, read a text, look at diagrams, view a film, examine real objects or any combination thereof.

Participation

The student's role is usually passive —reading the text or just listening to the teacher.	Modules provide for active student participation. The student learns by doing. The student is actively involved in manipulating the instructional materials.

Attribute

Conventional Lesson	*Module*

Achievement

Individual differences in achievement are expected. If a student wants enrichment materials, he usually must "dig" them out on his own. Tools and time for individual diagnosis and remedial help are normally lacking or not available. If a student is having difficulty, the teacher must work with him to help him keep up with the class or let him go and fend for himself.	A module is considered a failure if a significant number of students fail to reach the criterion performance. If a student wants to study a particular topic in greater depth, he can secure supplementary materials and proceed without interrupting the progress of an entire class. Remedial help and extra time are also available for slow learners to reach mastery. If a student is having difficulty mastering a lesson, he can spend the additional time and get individual help from the teacher without delaying the entire class.

Time

Time spent on a topic is usually constant for all learners which results in no time variance. Thus, achievement scores correlate highly with I.Q.	The students spend as much time as necessary to master the topic. Time required for mastery is usually distributed normally and tends to correlate highly with I.Q.

Freedom

Traditionally, forty-five minutes or an hour each day are scheduled at a fixed time for instruction. Students are forced to attend lectures and laboratories when they are in progress (e.g., from 8:00 to 8:50 on Monday, Wednesday and Friday).	Instruction can be at the student's convenience and at the time of day when the student learns "best." Modules provide greater freedom for students to adjust study time and subject matter content to individual needs and peculiarities of interest.

Reinforcement

In traditional courses, students are reinforced or corrected only after major examinations. Many times there is a considerable delay between the time when the exam is taken and when it is graded and returned to him.	The small size of the module permits immediate reinforcement and correction.

Conventional Lesson   *Module*

Testing

Tests usually sample the content which has been "covered." The student is often at a loss as to how to prepare (study) for the test. The student sits through the course, then takes an examination to determine his grade for the course. Tests are too often used only to "give grades," rather than for feedback or diagnosis.

Learners are given the objectives and told how attainment of them will be evaluated. Tests are designed to measure mastery of the objectives. The student receives credit when he can demonstrate mastery even if he has *not* gone through the module. Test items (questions) are used for assessing prerequisite skills, for diagnosing difficulties and for confirming mastery.

Reference

Norm-referenced tests are used where success is dependent upon the performance of others in the class.

Criterion-referenced tests are used where success of the student is independent of the performance of others using the module.

Mastery

Most learners know at least a little about everything. It is not expected that all students can achieve mastery.

Slow learners master some of the objectives but may not have time in an arbitrary period for other objectives. Given time, even slow learners can master most, if not all, of the objectives.

Portability

Conventional courses are usually based upon the teacher's lecture and are only portable by moving the teacher to a new location (sometimes accomplished via videotape). The lecture is usually lost forever after the class period ends. If a student misses part of a conventional course, he must talk with the teacher, review a fellow student's notes or miss the instruction entirely.

Modules can be portable and easily available at a variety of locations— in the field, at home or in a hospital. They can be easily exchanged and disseminated to other schools. Since the modules are in individual packages, make-up lessons and review sessions can be accommodated with a minimum of effort. All students are exposed to the same instruction, regardless of the hour of the day or the day of the week.

Attribute

Conventional Lesson   *Module*

Revisions

Revisions often reflect preferences of the teacher for content topics to be covered. Many times revisions necessitate a complete rewriting of the text or study guide and a major revision of all study material.

Revisions of materials are based on student performance. If students are not mastering material, it is revised. Subject matter which is constantly changing can be updated with a minimum of cost and effort.

Flexibility

Conventional courses are structured around a semester or year-long course outline or textbook and tend to be inflexible.

Modules can be structured into a greater variety of patterns consistent with different approaches or themes.

Course Success

Lacking the features of systematic design and specific objectives, there is no built-in provision for judging success of the course other than the teacher's subjective judgement.

Having a design goal and an evaluation plan, the module developer is able to correct faulty instructional materials and know when he has succeeded in developing a successful module.

Student Failure

Failure is usually not detected until the end of an examination period (six weeks or even a semester). Students often try to build hierarchical skills upon an inadequate foundation. Many times students are forced to repeat an entire semester or course.

Inadequate achievement can be identified at each critical step in the student's progress. Consequently, the subject matter is mastered before the student proceeds to subsequent studies. Failure can be pinpointed specifically to both subject matter and instructional material and subsequently remedied with a minimum of time and effort. The student has to repeat just that module which was failed, not an entire course.

CHAPTER III

Selection of Modules

After reading and studying this chapter, you should be able to:

1. *Describe the module selection process as outlined in Figure C.*
2. *Discuss the three alternatives for obtaining modules and identify the order in which they should be used.*
3. *Design a feasibility study for determining the possibility of using modules in your instructional situation.*
4. *Evaluate a given module using a checklist, such as the one presented in Figure D.*
5. *Outline the process for converting conventional materials to a modular format.*

Before one can effectively use modular materials in the classroom, it is necessary to go through the selection process which is outlined in Figure C. Basically, there are three alternatives as shown in the three columns of the figure:

1. The easiest and most desirable alternative is to locate relevant modules available for your use. These modules are then inspected using a checklist (as indicated in the left column).
2. If there are no relevant modules available, it is possible to modify existing materials and convert them to a modular format (as indicated in the right column).

3. The final alternative is to design new materials in the modular format (as indicated in the center column). Designing new materials is the most time consuming. Chapters IV through X describe in detail the design and development of modular materials.

FEASIBILITY STUDY

Early in the selection process non-academic factors should be considered. Does the module require elaborate and expensive hardware? Can the school afford to purchase enough of the tangibles and expendable supplies to meet enrollment needs? Are there learning center facilities available to accommodate the type of environment needed for modular instruction (individual study carrels, small group discussion areas and large group assembly rooms)? If tape recorders and projectors are to be used, maintenance costs must be considered in addition to the initial investment. What is the estimated cost per student hour of instruction? How does this compare with the cost of other teaching strategies?

A feasibility study should be conducted *before* any modular materials are adopted. The study should yield affirmative answers to the following questions:

1. Can acceptable patterns of scheduling group and individual activities be achieved?
2. Can acceptable arrangements be made for storing, scheduling and maintaining the equipment and other supplies?
3. Are costs in line with available funds? Consideration must be given to both initial and continuing costs for supplies, equipment, maintenance, supervision and facilities.

SELECTION

When it has been determined that it is feasible to consider modular instruction, the next step is to locate suitable modules by scanning bibliographies and lists of available modules. A module's initial suitability depends primarily upon the relevance of its subject matter, as well as on the complexity of its content and the time required for completion of the module. Of course, there are other factors that must be considered in the selection of modules. Specifically, how does the module fit into the curriculum? What student skills and knowledge are prerequisite? Modules not meeting these criteria are usually not considered. The alternatives are to develop your own modules or to modify existing materials into a modular format. (See Figure C.)

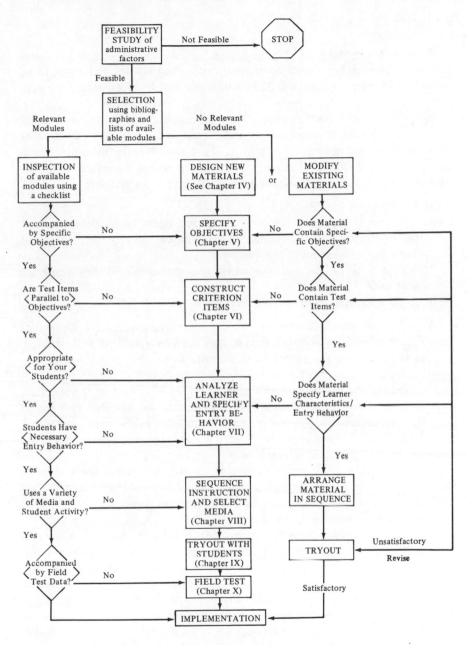

FIGURE C
The selection process.

INSPECTION

The relevant modules are then inspected using a checklist, such as the one in Figure D. The teacher should actually examine the modules that seem to be suitable. Particular attention should be paid to the stated objectives and the field test data.

A checklist may be used to estimate the educational potential of the modules under consideration. In selecting modules for use in the classroom, the teacher must consider his objectives as well as his students' entry behavior. These characteristics of the instructional situation must be compared with the objectives and difficulty of the module. It is helpful to have available:

1. A copy of the module
2. A statement regarding the prerequisite knowledge (entry behavior) and learner characteristics of the intended population
3. The specific objectives of the module
4. A description of how and with whom (target population) the module has been used
5. A statistical evaluation of the field test results.

A module complete with the above information is rarely available. Generally, only the module itself is available, thus making it the only basis for evaluation. A careful inspection of the module may indicate its possible effectiveness with your students.

As shown in the left column of Figure C, you need to look at the checklist (Figure D) and the module and ask, "Is the module accompanied by a list of specific objectives?" If it is, you are ready to move on to the next step. If not and if you decide to use the module, you will need to write some objectives for the module as described in Chapter V.

Now you should check any test items which may accompany the module to determine whether they adequately measure the objectives. If they do not, you can refer to Chapter VI on the construction of criterion items.

The next consideration is whether the module is suitable for *your* students and whether the students have the necessary entry behavior. Basically, you need to ask, "Is the language level appropriate and is the content interesting to the students?" An important question to ask is "Does the module have 'student appeal'?" Does the student suffer because of a monotonous presentation or impersonal style? Is the learner actively involved with the module? Interpersonal reaction is important in every learning situation, even if the "tutor" is a book or an audiotape. An abundant sprinkling of "you's" and "we's" adds to the module's appeal. Pictures and humor also should be used effectively to increase student appeal. The selection of media and sequencing of content are also important in your inspection of a module for possible classroom use. It is also necessary to check the quality of the module's subject matter content. Is the treatment of the subject matter accurate and up-to-date? Does the author make serious mistakes or omissions of fact or theory? Is the organization and instructional sequence clear? Is there adequate discussion involved in the introduction of new concepts and technical terms? If you are not a subject matter specialist, you should consult one for the answers to questions such as these. Many of the questions you ask this specialist will be similar to the questions you yourself have asked about the module; however, he may look at the module from a different point of view and provide additional insight into the probable quality and effectiveness of the material.

Finally, is the module accompanied by validation or field test data? If so and if the results meet your satisfaction, you are ready to seriously consider adding the module to your curriculum. If not, a field test should be conducted under actual learning conditions with a group of your students as described in Chapter X.

Potential users cannot always reliably assess the effectiveness of a module by just inspecting it. Several studies[1] have shown a high *negative* correlation between "effectiveness ratings" obtained from a panel of "experts" and the experimental evidence from field testing. In other words, those materials which the experts *thought* to be superior were inferior when actually used with students. Therefore, to verify the consequences of using a module in a particular teaching situation, the teacher should try out the material on a limited basis before large-scale adoption. The group of students used for field testing should include the ability range of those students who will use the module if it is adopted—don't use just your best students! Evidence for the effectiveness of a module or modular sequence should be based on a carefully conducted study which shows the module's use under specific conditions. Such a study should use suitable pretest and posttest measurements as described in Chapter X. Evaluation under field test conditions forces the module to speak for itself! How well does it teach what it is supposed to teach?

CONVERTING CONVENTIONAL MATERIALS TO MODULES

If there are no relevant modules in your subject matter area which seem appropriate for your students, an alternative is to convert existing, conventional materials into a modular format as indicated in the right column of Figure C.

You can divide your course into smaller, more manageable units. It is suggested that each module require not more than a few hours of student time

---

[1]E. Z. Rothkopf, "Some Observations on Predicting Instructional Effectiveness by Simple Inspection," *Journal of Programmed Instruction* (Summer, 1963), pp. 19-20.

to complete. If you are using a textbook for the course, the chapters may be an acceptable core for the modules. If the chapters are too lengthy, sub-sections of chapters may be used.

Once the content of the module has been identified, you must ask, "Does the material contain stated objectives?" If not, you will need to write objectives for that content as described in Chapter V. From the objectives, you can design test items to measure mastery of the objectives (see Chapter VI) if they are not provided in the text or the teacher's manual.

Objectives

1. Is the module accompanied by a list of objectives stated in specific behavioral terms (i.e., student performance terms, performance conditions and acceptable performance standards)?

Test Items

2. Does the posttest measure the student's comprehension of the objectives of the module?

Entry Behavior

3. Is the module accompanied by a description of the target population (entry behavior and learner characteristics)?
   Is the module appropriate for your students?
   Do your students have the necessary entry behavior?

Media

4. Does the module use a variety of media (visuals, audiotapes, books, films and actual materials when and where appropriate)?
   Does the student have the option of using as many senses as possible (visual, audio, tactile, smell and taste)?
   Are real materials handled by the student whenever possible?

Content

5. Is the treatment of the subject matter accurate and up-to-date?
   Is the organization and instructional sequence clear and logical?

Field Test Data

6. Is the module accompanied by validation data including the following?
   a. Target population (entry behavior and learner characteristics)
   b. Instructional situation
   c. Time taken to complete module
   d. Gain in student achievement
   e. Changes in student attitude

Figure D
Brief checklist for evaluating modular materials.

It is important to specify the entry behavior and learner characteristics for the material. Few commercially available materials contain this type of information, so you will probably need to do this yourself as outlined in Chapter VII.

You may want to supplement the content in the textbook or other reference with media such as audiotapes, films, filmstrips or colored slides. It is also possible to build a module around a film or filmstrip. You will need to arrange the material in a sequence which will allow the students to master the objectives (see Chapter IX).

If the achievement is satisfactory and the students relate positively to the module, your conversion job is finished. Usually, it is necessary to make minor modifications and revisions of the module based on student tryout. You may need to rewrite the objectives until they communicate your instructional intent to the students. Often, the test items must be rephrased so that they accurately measure student learning. With a little effort and creativity, the materials will allow your students to meet the objectives.

It is usually less costly in terms of both time and money to develop modules from existing materials, rather than "to start from scratch." There is no justification for inventing the wheel! However, for certain subject matter areas and grade levels, there may be no existing materials which are appropriate. In this case, it is necessary to design your own materials. Chapters IV through X describe the design and development process in detail.

SUMMARY

The selection of modules should begin with a feasibility study to determine whether it is possible and practical to use modules in your instructional situation. If affirmative, you then need to select potential modules and evaluate them using criteria such as those given in this chapter. If no suitable modules are available, it may be possible to convert conventional materials into modular format. Another possibility is to design your own materials as described in the next chapter.

CHAPTER IV

Designing Modules:
An Overview

After reading and studying this chapter, you should be able to:

1. *List in order the six steps used in the design and development of modules. Your answer should include a brief description of each step.*
2. *Diagram the interrelation of the six steps in the development process.*
3. *Apply this systematic approach in the development of multi-media modules.*

The systematic approach for the design, development and validation of modular instruction involves six interrelated steps.

1. Exact specification of objectives
2. Construction of criterion items
3. Analysis of learner characteristics and specification of entry behavior
4. Sequencing of instruction and selection of media
5. Student tryout of the module
6. Evaluation of the module

This chapter presents a brief introduction to these six steps and develops a simple model (flowchart) that shows the relationship between the components. The model offers a logical structure and an orderly application of proven instructional strategies for designing modules and making educational decisions. Chapters V through X describe each of the steps in detail and offer practical suggestions and techniques for the development of modules.

EXACT SPECIFICATION OF OBJECTIVES

The objectives of a module are specifications of what the student should be able to do after completing the module. Technically, we will call this *terminal behavior.* If the student can not perform to those specifications, then either the objectives need to be changed or the instructional approach within the module must be changed. The instructional material, not the student, has failed.

This process can be represented diagrammatically as follows:

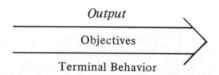

Only if we clearly identify the terminal behavior can we adequately determine what has to be done, by what or by whom, to meet the learning objectives. The application of a systematic approach to the development of modules makes it possible to ensure that the objectives (terminal behaviors) will be met by a majority of the students.

CONSTRUCTION OF CRITERION ITEMS

If we are going to be able to objectively determine whether or not the student has mastered the objectives, we must have a valid test to measure his acquisition of the required behavior. The criterion test or posttest will serve as a decision point both in the design of the module and in the evaluation during its use.

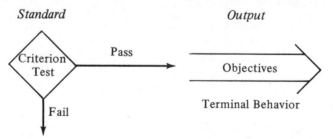

During the design of the module, the criterion test will assist the developer in locating weak portions of the instruction which need to be modified until they are effective. Once the module is in use, the posttest results will serve a diagnostic function for the student and allow him to pinpoint weaknesses or omissions in his learning.

ANALYSIS OF LEARNER CHARACTERISTICS AND SPECIFICATION OF ENTRY BEHAVIOR

Usually, the student begins the module with some skills, information and/or competencies which are relevant to what he is supposed to learn. We usually refer to relevant competencies which the learner brings to the learning experience as the *entry behavior* of the learner. Since it would be a waste of time and effort to "teach" competencies that the learner already possesses, it is the job of the instructional developer to determine what related capabilities the student has already acquired.

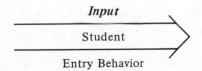

Input

Student

Entry Behavior

By constructing and using an *entry test*, we can determine what a student already knows about a topic or process. Of course, this will vary from one student to another, and consideration of this variation is highly important. It is usually advisable to set a minimum entry behavior. The student who has not already acquired these minimum capabilities will be frustrated and will probably fail. On the other hand, the student who has to go through material he already knows is going to be bored and will probably lose interest. A test of entry behavior will help to minimize learning problems caused by both extremes.

SEQUENCING OF INSTRUCTION AND SELECTION OF MEDIA

The selection and sequencing of the media are important in order to optimize the organization and presentation of the instructional materials and resources. Media include textbooks, photographs, films, equipment, audiotapes and other resources. The purpose of the media is to assist the student in mastering the stated objectives.

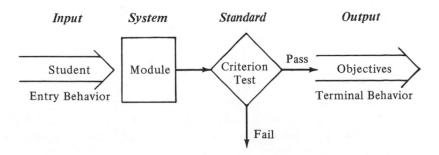

The module should provide as much direct experience with the objects being studied as possible. There are few, if any, axioms which tell the developer exactly what he should use and no formula which specifies in what proportions the ingredients should be mixed. Many of these decisions are dependent upon the expertise of the subject-matter specialist. Therefore, it is often advisable to consult several subject-matter specialists and instructional developers for their opinions.

STUDENT TRYOUT OF THE MODULE

The best criterion by which the effectiveness of modules can be evaluated is the extent to which the student masters the objectives. Thus, the performance of the student is evaluated to assess the degree to which the system has facilitated student achievement. Furthermore, the student's performance on a criterion test at the end of instruction will provide "feedback" (information used to correct any discrepancy between what the student is doing and what he should be doing) to both the student and the instructional developer.

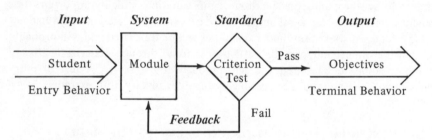

The responsibility for learning is placed upon the individual student, but, if a sizeable portion of the students fail to achieve the terminal behavior, it is probably a fault of the instruction and not the students. During student tryout, students go through the module and provide feedback—written responses, verbal comments and non-verbal gestures. After the necessary revisions have been made, another group of students goes through the learning experience and their feedback is used to further improve the system. The test-revision cycle is used again and again until the students' performance meets the criterion set forth in the objectives.

EVALUATION OF THE MODULE

The purpose of evaluation is to check the effectiveness of the module. A group of students goes through the material and their performance is carefully measured to determine the effectiveness of the module. When it is not possible to conduct extensive testing, a checklist (as described in Chapter III) can be used to estimate the effectiveness of the module.

A module can also be evaluated by the resources that are required. In other words, the economy of the instructional package is another criterion by which it can be assessed. The goal of all instruction is to attain the objectives with the least expenditure of time, energy and resources—optimization of instruction.

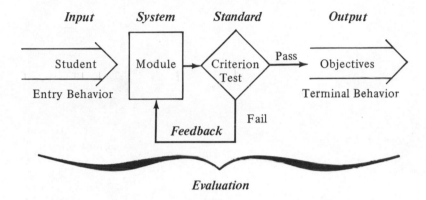

Evaluation

Even after the module has been validated by extensive testing, the developer needs to monitor the performance of the students working with the material and to make necessary revisions if the students do not meet the objectives of the module.

SUMMARY

Designing modules is a *dynamic* process. Even though it has been represented and discussed here as a step-by-step sequence from exact specification of objectives to evaluation of the module, it is in reality a continuous process. The procedure need not be followed one step at a time even though the recommended sequence has been found to be most helpful for novices in the development process. This process is highly interactive, with each step having an effect on the preceding steps as well as those that follow it. For example, in the fourth step (Sequencing of Instruction), you may find it necessary to go back and modify your objectives or change the entry behavior requirements.

The following chapters will discuss each of the six steps of the design process in detail. First, we will examine the most important component of a module, namely the instructional objectives. A bad start here can necessitate a lot of additional time later or result in the scrapping of the entire module. Spend a lot of time formulating and carefully delineating the objectives for your module.

CHAPTER V

Exact Specification
of Objectives

After reading and studying this chapter, you should be able to:

1. *Discuss three purposes of the exact specification of objectives.*
2. *Given any topic, state objectives which contain performance terms, performance conditions and a statement of acceptable performance.*
3. *Analyze a general objective in your subject matter field and specify the necessary sub-objectives.*
4. *Classify any cognitive objective into one of the six levels of Bloom's taxonomy.*

Specifying objectives is the initial—and essential—stage in the design and development of any instructional material. When you can specify the objectives for your module, you have overcome the biggest hurdle in instructional development.

Specific objectives serve three purposes. For the instructional developer, they are valuable in planning and sequencing the instructional activities, as well as in evaluating their effectiveness. For other teachers, they give insight into the suitability of the module for their students and aid in the design of tests for evaluation of student performance. For the student, they describe exactly what is expected of him and provide him with a goal to be mastered. Hence, the student's learning activities become goal-oriented.

To be useful to different people (instructional developers, other teachers and students), objectives *must* convey the same meaning to each person. There should be no question in interpretation such as "What does this objective really mean?"

The purpose of specifying objectives is to increase the clarity of the level of performance to be reached by the student. Vague objectives create confusion and uncertainty which defeat the main purpose of stating objectives. The more specifically and clearly a behavior is defined, the easier it is to tell if that behavior is being expressed. Objectives also tell how well and under what conditions the student must perform.

Objectives exist on a continuum from extremely non-behavioral and vague to very specific.

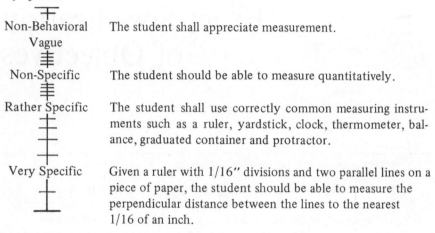

Non-Behavioral   The student shall appreciate measurement.
Vague

Non-Specific   The student should be able to measure quantitatively.

Rather Specific   The student shall use correctly common measuring instruments such as a ruler, yardstick, clock, thermometer, balance, graduated container and protractor.

Very Specific   Given a ruler with 1/16" divisions and two parallel lines on a piece of paper, the student should be able to measure the perpendicular distance between the lines to the nearest 1/16 of an inch.

Robert Mager[1] suggests that to be extremely clear and specific, an instructional objective should:

1. Be stated in performance terms.
2. Give the conditions under which the performance should occur.
3. Include a statement of acceptable performance.

We will look at the parts of specific objectives beginning with the behavioral or performance terms.

"The student shall know the parts of the microscope."

"The student shall really understand the microscope."

To "know" and to "really understand" signify different things to different people. Naming the parts of a microscope, recognizing the parts on a drawing,

---

[1] R. F. Mager, *Preparing Instructional Objectives* (Palo Alto, Calif.: Fearon Publishers, 1962), p. 53.

listing the uses of the microscope, reciting the optical principles which explain how the microscope magnifies—all involve knowing or understanding the microscope to varying degrees.

Robert Mager[2] identifies words open to many interpretations and those open to fewer interpretations.

Many Interpretations

to know	to grasp the significance of
to understand	to enjoy
to really understand	to believe
to appreciate	to have faith in
to fully appreciate	to feel

Few Interpretations

to write	to construct
to recite	to list
to identify	to compare
to differentiate	to contrast
to solve	to diagram

Going back to our example with the microscope, a general indication of student performance would be: "The student shall be able to operate a microscope." Now we know what the student should be able to do, but we still do not understand under what conditions he is expected to operate the microscope or with what degree of proficiency.

Next, let us examine some conditions under which a student could be expected to perform. Here are three additional objectives which might be used in a module:

"The student shall analyze the causes of World War II."

"The student shall hit a golf ball."

"The student shall translate a passage of French."

Even though these objectives contain behavioral terms (analyze, hit and translate), they are not as specific as they could be. They do *not* indicate the *conditions* under which the student is to perform. For example, the first objective does not specify what type of references or information the student is allowed to use in analyzing the causes of World War II.

"Given a list of ten possible causes of World War II but without reference to his textbook, the student shall analyze the causes of World War II and rank them as to probable importance and justify the ranking."

[2]*Ibid.*, p. 11.

The conditions should define specifically the range of problems the student is expected to solve. If the student is to identify birds, what birds should he be able to name on sight? All birds? In the birds' natural habitat? From colored pictures in a book?

The second objective does not indicate what equipment the student is to use or where he is to hit the ball. Must he hit it a certain distance?

"Given a golf club (#1 wood), a tee and ball, the student will drive the ball off the tee at least 200 yards and keep it on the fairway in four out of five attempts."

Thus, the conditions should also identify what equipment or aids and particularly what references the student may or may not use to meet the objective.

"Without the aid of his textbook, the student shall translate any simple equation (in terms of two variables) into the correct slope-intercept form and plot it accurately on standard graph paper."

"Given a thermometer, the student shall record the temperature of two containers of liquid (one painted black and the other silver)."

The third objective does not indicate under what conditions the student shall translate the passage. What type of passage is he expected to translate? Can he use a dictionary?

"With the aid of a French-English dictionary, the student shall translate into English a 200-word passage from a French newspaper."

Selecting the proper qualifying terms or acceptable performance is the most difficult part of writing objectives. In other words, what must the student do to meet your criteria? In some situations, the speed with which the student performs is critical (for instance, translating Morse code or typing). In most learning, however, the time limit is not a critical factor.

The tolerance or permitted range of errors is often important. If the student is measuring an object, how accurately should his result be? To the nearest inch or to the nearest sixteenth of an inch? If the student is measuring the width of his desk, you may be satisfied if he is accurate to the nearest inch. On the other hand, you might want him to be within a sixteenth of an inch in his measurement of the width of his pencil.

Usually, it is important to list the proportion or percentage of correct responses required to meet your standards of performance. If the student is solving math problems, what percentage should be solved correctly for mastery? Ninety percent, eight out of ten or all of them?

Following is a checklist which should be helpful when you begin writing objectives. Not all the conditions or standards may be applicable, but make your objectives as specific as possible.

Rate your objectives with this checklist.[3]

CHECKLIST FOR EVALUATING OBJECTIVES

Performance

1. Does the objective contain a statement of the required student behavior?

Performance Conditions

2. Does it contain a statement of each of the following types of conditions (if applicable)?
   A. Range of problems which the student is expected to handle.
   B. Equipment, tools, aids and references which the student may or may not use.
   C. Special environmental conditions in which the student has to perform.

Acceptable Performance

3. Does it contain a statement of each of the following types of standards required of the student's performance (if applicable)?
   A. Time limit.
   B. Permitted tolerance (accuracy) for the student's responses.
   C. The proportion or percentage of correct responses required.

As indicated earlier in this chapter, objectives range from non-behavioral and vague to very specific. Some instructional developers and teachers do not specify objectives in minute detail. Instead, they use "less than perfect" objectives. The important consideration is whether intent of the objectives, regardless of their format, is communicated to the students. Even if your objectives meet all the criteria in the checklist given previously but do not communicate accurately your intentions to your students, then they are worthless! The final judgement on any objective must be determined by its usefulness to the teacher, the developer and, most importantly, the students.

When you have decided on the general objective(s) for your module, you need to determine the prerequisite behaviors necessary for achieving your objective(s). One technique for analyzing a learning task is to work backwards from the most to the least complex behavior which the student should develop in the lesson. For example, by analyzing a complex behavior to determine the necessary subordinate or prerequisite behaviors, it is possible to construct a hierarchy that begins with the most simple behaviors necessary for the attainment of the general objective.

"Given a Bausch and Lomb elementary school microscope (Model

---

[3] S. Thiagarajan, *Programmed Programming* (Bloomington, Indiana: author, 1969).

ESM-100) and a prepared slide, the students will set up the microscope, adjust the mirror and focus an image of the slide. Acceptable performance will be the attainment of a bright, clear and sharp image of the prepared slide."

You then analyze the general objective and decide which more specific behaviors are involved in mastering the general objective. The more specific behavior can be called a sub-objective. Let's now analyze the general objective stated above and determine the sub-objectives.

"Given the Bausch and Lomb elementary school microscope (Model ESM-100) and a prepared slide, the student should be able to:

adjust the mirror to provide the most effective use of the available light in the field of vision.

focus the object on the prepared slide into clear, sharp focus using ample light.

place the slide on the stage so that it is held by the stage clips and the object to be viewed is in the center of the hole on the stage.

lower the lens with the coarse adjustment knob while viewing from the side (not through the eyepiece) until the objective almost touches the slide.

raise the lens with the coarse adjustment knob until the slide to be viewed comes almost into focus when observed through the eyepiece.

move the lens into final adjustment using the fine adjustment knob.

handle the microscope with proper care when getting it out and putting it away (carry it with one hand holding the arm of the microscope and the other hand holding the base).

name and identify the twelve most frequently used parts of the microscope with ninety percent accuracy. The parts to be named are base, pillar, arm, stage, stage clip, fine adjustment knob, coarse adjustment knob, mirror, lens, nosepiece, body tube and eyepiece."

As you can see, the number of sub-objectives depends upon the difficulty of the general objective.

Benjamin S. Bloom and a team of educators[4] developed a taxonomy for classifying cognitive objectives. The cognitive levels are:

6. Evaluation	3. Application
5. Synthesis	2. Comprehension
4. Analysis	1. Knowledge

---

[4] Benjamin S. Bloom, et al., *Taxonomy of Educational Objectives: Cognitive Domain* (New York: David McKay Company, 1956).

Each level from knowledge upward is progressively more complex than the one below it and therefore builds upon it.

Knowledge objectives involve recall of information such as stating the date of an event, telling what 3 times 5 equals, spelling a word correctly or naming the parts of an object. Also included at this level is performance of a simple task such as reading a poem, finding the location of a city on a map, calculating the answer to a long division problem or adjusting a microscope. This type of objective requires minimal organization of information and therefore is easily forgotten. However, it is necessary to build upon it for the higher levels.

Comprehension objectives include translating, interpreting and extrapolating information. Translation involves changing information into a different symbolic form or language without loss of accuracy of the original content. Examples would be drawing a picture to illustrate a story, reading a verbal problem statement and illustrating it with concrete objects or describing a given process in the student's own words. Interpreting data or information is exemplified by answering a question from data presented on a graph, explaining the meaning of a folk song or demonstrating with a globe and flashlight the cycle of nights and days on the earth. Extrapolation relates to the ability to extend the meaning of major ideas beyond the limits of the information presented. Typical extrapolation activities are predicting the value of the y-coordinate for a given x-coordinate beyond the limits of a line graph or making a general statement about the need for air pollution control after studying its present level and effects.

Application objectives require ability to use ideas, principles and theories in particular concrete situations. The student must identify the concept, principle or idea involved and then *apply* it correctly. It involves transfer of training. An example is the description of what Indiana would be like if it were an island, or using facts about known animals to make inferences about another animal not studied or applying the relationship between heat and the expansion and contraction of liquids to explain how a thermometer works.

Anaylsis objectives involve breaking down an idea into its component parts and determining the relationship between the parts. Examples include determining which statements about an experiment are facts and which are hypotheses, stating which quotations from a play are inconsistent or locating the problems with a malfunctioning mechanical device.

Synthesis objectives include putting together parts and elements to form a new whole or pattern. The student uses concepts, principles or ideas already learned to make a novel product. Examples are the use of the results of a survey to plan a course of action, the sequencing of an instructional unit after developing each of the individual parts or suggestions for possible treatments for a disease based upon facts about the disease.

Evaluation objectives, the highest of the six levels in the cognitive domain, require making judgements. They include only judgements based upon specific criteria and do not include opinions. Examples are evaluating popular beliefs about dieting using physiological data as the criteria, judging a bulletin board on the basis of a set of given criteria or discussing the most efficient way to reduce noise level in a factory to meet present government standards.

The taxonomy of cognitive objectives is useful as a guide to determine whether a module covers a broad range of abilities. It is very easy to fall into the trap of teaching only low level (knowledge and comprehension) objectives. You should analyse your objectives to be certain that many, if not all, of the levels are represented.

After the objectives for your module are complete, you know where you want the students to go, and they know your target. Next, you will need to devise a means of determining when the students have "arrived" or mastered the objectives for your module.

SUMMARY

Well-written performance objectives:

1. Specify student competencies to be gained from the module.
2. Assist teachers in the selection and evaluation of the module.
3. Guide the developer in the design of the module.

The chapter provides samples of properly written objectives and a checklist for evaluating objectives. An example of an analysis of a complex terminal objective into a series of sub-objectives is included.

CHAPTER VI

Construction of Criterion Items

After reading and studying this chapter, you should be able to:

1. *Define and give examples of the following:*
   a. *Parallel items*
   b. *Relevant questions*
   c. *Critical questions*
   d. *Student behavior*
   e. *Student products*
   f. *Criterion items*
2. *Given an objective, construct a criterion item which measures mastery of the objective. The item should be constructed within the guidelines presented in this chapter.*
3. *Differentiate between "norm-referenced" and "criterion-referenced" evaluation and give an example of each.*

To determine whether or not the student has mastered the objectives for your module, you must measure the student's performance. Your objectives should set the level of performance which is acceptable for your module, thus giving you and your students guidelines for the desired behavior. Evaluation conducted at different stages of the lesson can disclose progress as well as problems for the students and the teacher.

You have stated your objectives for the module in terms of observable and therefore measurable performance. The next step is to construct a test situation for each of these objectives. Since the purpose of this test is primarily to determine whether the student has met the performance standard or criterion for the module and not to give him a grade, the test is called a "criterion test."

Before the student begins the module, pretest items may be used to measure how much the student already knows about the topic. Questions and performance within the module will assist the developer in locating ineffective portions of the instruction which need to be revised and improved. The criterion items also help the student evaluate his own progress. The posttest items, given after completion of the module, can determine whether the student has mastered the material. In addition, they can serve a diagnostic function and allow the student to pinpoint weaknesses or omissions in his learning.

For an elementary science module on classification, the objective might be: "Given a collection of objects (or pictures of objects), the student should be able to classify the objects according to a single characteristic which has been specified by someone else." The criterion item would simply be to give the child a set of different colored wooden blocks and ask him to separate them according to color. This is a specific criterion item corresponding to a particular objective.

If there are three objectives for the modules, there should be at least three test items in a one-to-one correspondence.

> Objective A . . . . . . Test Item A
> Objective B . . . . . . Test Item B
> Objective C . . . . . . Test Item C

The instructor can then assemble one of the test items for each of the objectives and form the posttest. Since the posttest represents the standard for student achievement, it is the quality check for the module. If the student does not achieve at a satisfactory level, the developer and/or student can analyze the items missed to determine omissions in the student's learning and weaknesses in the instructional materials.

Many instructors prefer to have alternate forms of the posttest, so it would be helpful to have several parallel forms of the test questions. A parallel test item measures the same behavioral objective but uses a different situation or set of information. For an objective on analyzing the plot of a short story, the parallel item would ask the student to analyze the plot of a different short story. The reason for using different specimens or different data in the question is to avoid rote memorization of the answers to the questions. Often, we will want to check the student's progress as he works through the module. The student also appreciates an indication of his success with the material. To do this, we may include parallel test items within the module itself which he can use as a self-check.

Some instructors like to pretest their students to determine how much of the material they have learned before beginning the module. Parallel forms of the test items are also helpful for these people. In constructing the pretest, the developer can use the same criterion items or parallel items which measure the same behavioral objectives but use a different situation or set of information.

There is no rule prescribing the number of test questions which should be developed for each objective, but at least three would be desirable—one for the pretest, one for the posttest and one for use within the module. Some objectives, such as the ability to operate a piece of machinery or equipment, have just one possible test item (namely the proper operation of the machine), and it can be used in all evaluation situations.

There are several guidelines which should be considered in constructing questions for modules. The questions must be *relevant*, that is, related to the objectives of the module and pertinent to their purpose. For example, if the objective states that the student should be able to parallel park an automobile, the evaluation should require him to actually perform the maneuver. Just asking the student to describe the process is irrelevant to the objective. Therefore, to check the relevancy of a question, one must compare it to the objective it is designed to measure.

The questions should require the learner to use the most important information presented in the module. *Critical* questions focus the student's attention on the most important material because he needs to apply this information when giving the answer. In order to maintain a flow of information, some subject matter is presented for continuity, but it may not be important for meeting the objectives. In a module on the planets, you may mention that Pluto is 3,670,000,000 miles from the sun even though you do not expect the student to remember this fact. The critical information may be that Pluto is the farthest known planet from the sun.

Modules usually lend themselves to two types of evaluation—*student products* and *student demonstrations*. Student products could include a piece of sculpture, student-made diagrams, artistic drawings or a written description of what the student did during an experiment. The answers to more traditional test items also fall within this category. On the other hand, student demonstrations include observable activities like the student's ability to classify objects or to serve a tennis ball properly. In all cases, the teacher must observe the student behavior as it progresses. A student product can be evaluated at a later time. The type of test used—product or demonstration—depends upon the corresponding objective which the test item is measuring.

Test items custom-made for a particular module provide the advantage of measuring the specific objectives of that module. The test constructor must know the merits and weaknesses of each type of test item. Here are a few guidelines for question construction compiled by the author.

GENERAL GUIDELINES

1. The test item must measure a stated objective in order to be valid. The test also should discriminate between the student who has met the objective and the student who has not.

For the following objective,

"Given the annual population statistics for any period of time, the student should be able to plot a graph showing the relationship between time and population grcwth."

an inappropriate test item would be a true-false question referring to a graph of time and population.

"The graph above shows the relationship between time and population growth." True or false.

Another improper evaluation question for the objective given above would be a multiple-choice question designed to determine the student's understanding of the causes of fluctuation in population growth. The only appropriate and valid way to measure this objective is to give the student a set of annual population statistics and ask him to actually draw a graph of these data.

2. Clear and complete instructions for answering or performing each item should be provided. Otherwise, the student may miss the acceptable performance level just because the instructions are not properly stated. Each test item should describe clearly what the student is to do.

3. The type of criterion item used to evaluate a specific objective should be appropriate for that objective. There are many different types of test items—multiple-choice, matching, completion, short answer, true-false and actual performance (student behavior) items. You should choose the type which best measures the desired student response. Avoid using only one kind of test item throughout the module.

4. The vocabulary level of the test should be appropriately matched to the range of ability of the students. Otherwise, language difficulties may prevent the student from demonstrating mastery of the objective.

True-False

1. Avoid long and involved statements since they tend to confuse the student who actually could answer the question but is distracted by the complexity of the sentence.

2. If the statement is false, it should be incorrect because a major part of the sentence is incorrect and not because a minute, inconspicuous detail slipped into the sentence makes it incorrect. An example of a poor true-false item is:

"The Wright brothers tested the first full-sized, power-driven airplane at Kitty Hawk, South Carolina, in 1903." (The correct statement should include *North* Carolina not South Carolina—a rather trivial point!)

3. Never use a double negative. In fact, it is advisable to make the statement positive.

4. Restrict each statement to a single idea or principle. Items with several parts are often confusing.

5. Base items on key ideas and objectives and avoid the use of statements taken directly from the module.

Multiple-Choice

1. The stem of the item should be clear, and it should present a single idea to be completed.

2. Each of the possible responses should provide a logical completion of the stem for uninformed students who have not mastered the objective.

3. You should avoid idiosyncratic clues, such as always making the correct answer the longest or the most-detailed choice or having a plural verb in the stem and only one plural form among the alternatives. An example of a poor question is:

"Which of these men were explorers of the Louisiana Territory?
A. Richard Byrd
B. Lewis and Clark
C. Daniel Boone
D. Thomas Jefferson"

4. There should be only one correct or "best" response to complete the stem.

5. The stem should state fully the central question and all choices should be correct grammatically.

Matching

1. The instructions should indicate the basis for matching and state whether an answer may be used more than once and whether more than one answer is to be given for any of the questions.

2. Every choice in the second column should be a possible match for the first column.

3. There should be extra choices in the answer column to avoid selection by the process of elimination.

4. All items in each column of a matching question should be homogeneous, i.e., of the same type—names, dates, elements, etc.

5. There should be from eight to twelve associations in each question,

depending upon the level of the student. An example of a poor matching question is:

MATCHING

___A. Country bordering Texas on the south	1. 1945
___B. First president of the United States	2. Revolution
___C. Year that the United Nations was formed	3. Washington
___D. Italian dictator during World War II	4. Russia
___E. Country launching first satellite	5. Mexico
___F. The overthrow of government by those governed	6. Mussolini

An example of a good matching question is:

Match the author's name given in the second column with his novel listed in column one. Use each author's number only once and place only one author's number in each blank.

NOVELS	AUTHORS
___A. The Last of the Mohicans	1. Mark Twain
___B. The Scarlet Letter	2. Louisa May Alcott
___C. Moby Dick	3. Nathaniel Hawthorne
___D. Huckleberry Finn	4. William Dean Howells
___E. The Rise of Silas Lapham	5. Robert Louis Stevenson
___F. Treasure Island	6. James Fenimore Cooper
___G. Little Women	7. Henry James
___H. A Farewell to Arms	8. John Steinbeck
	9. Herman Melville
	10. Ernest Hemingway

Completion

1. Avoid taking statements directly from the textbook or module because of the tendency to encourage students to just memorize key statements.

2. The blank(s) should be placed as close to the end of the statement as possible. Thus, by the time the student reaches the blank, he should understand the nature of the question being asked.

3. The length of the blanks should be the same to avoid giving an unnecessary clue as to the length of the correct answer.

4. Avoid a "Swiss cheese" item with too many blanks so that the intent of the statement is unclear. The first sentence is an example of a poor completion item; the second is a good example.

"_____ was the first man to _____ in _____."

"The highest level Indian civilization in America was achieved by the _____."

5. The statement should be worded so that only key words are omitted and so that there is only one correct response for each blank. The first example is a poor one; the second is a good example.

"The treaty ending the Civil War was signed in _____."(Any of the following would be correct: 1864, Appomatox or the mid-1860's.)

"The capital of Indiana is _____."

6. Do not give the answer away with grammatical clues. The second example is preferable to the first.

"A triangle with three equal sides is an _____ triangle."

"A triangle with three equal sides is a(n) _____ triangle."

Short Answer

1. The question should be as specific as possible. If the question is too general, the student who knows the subject may miss the answer because he writes on the wrong portion of a broad subject.

2. Avoid emphasis on specific facts or processes.

3. Encourage thinking or problem solving activities when possible.

4. Provide a model response or key words which the student or instructor can use to evaluate the answer objectively.

"What is an ohmmeter?" (Too broad a question—the student could describe its construction, its use or the electronic theory behind its operation.)

"Diagram the circuit of an ohmmeter." (A good short answer question.)

Actual Performance

1. Specify exactly what the student is to do, which equipment and materials he will be allowed to use and tell him how his performance is going to be evaluated.

2. A checklist can be used effectively to evaluate a performance. The checklist can be utilized either by the student or the instructor.

3. The student's performance may also be evaluated by examining a product of the performance.

4. Immediate feedback should be available to the student for self-instruction, reinforcement, evaluation and/or correction.

Essay

1. Use *several* fairly *specific* and *brief* questions rather than a few lengthy,

more general ones. The items should be general enough to offer some latitude but specific enough to set limits.

2. Limit each item to one idea or area of knowledge.

3. Provide structure in the item so the student knows exactly what is expected in his answer.

4. Focus on the higher level objectives (analysis, synthesis and evaluation) in essay questions.

"Discuss the causes of the Second World War." (Note that no specific directions for answering the question are given.)

"Analyze in about 1000 words three examples of authoritarian behavior demonstrated by Franklin Delano Roosevelt during his presidency of the United States. Your discussion should include: (1) the definition of authoritarianism, (2) three examples and (3) a rationale for Roosevelt's actions." (Note the similarity of this item to a well-written objective.)

5. When grading essay items, don't let your impressions of the student or his previous performance affect your grading of the answer. Keep the names anonymous until the items have been graded. Grade one question on all papers before going on to the next question. Use a scoring key with model answers and a point system.

USE OF CRITERION ITEMS

Criterion test items fall into two categories—constructed response and selected response. A multiple-choice question requires a selected response, while an essay item calls for a constructed response. It is important to use a wide variety of question formats. Direct questions, fill-in items, multiple-choice, matching, manipulation of equipment, drawing figures—each has appropriate circumstances in which it can be best utilized. A wide variety of questions helps to maintain student interest and also affords the opportunity to apply the information learned to a variety of situations.

The questions should require the student to understand and apply the information presented in the module. Many times, sentence structure provides a clue to the correct answer of a multiple-choice question. Some poorly written questions merely ask him to analyze unintentional clues or hints given in the question. This unintentional prompting is less likely to occur when performance items are used.

Modules can be graded in a number of different ways. First, the student can be evaluated on a pass-fail basis. If he meets all of the criterion items at the acceptable performance level, he receives a pass grade for the module and is ready to go on to new materials. On the other hand, if he does not reach the criterion performance standard, he must review or redo the materials until he can demonstrate mastery. If the student continues to have difficulty, the instructor should assist him on an individual basis.

Instructors who must give letter grades can evaluate the posttest in a traditional manner and assign grades accordingly. However, the author does not believe this approach is using the philosophy of modules to its best advantage. Modules and their evaluation should be *criterion-referenced*. That is, the student should be attempting to meet a standard or a level of acceptable performance rather than trying to be in the upper ten percent of the class in order to get an A. In the latter case, when the student is compared with a group, the test is said to be *norm-referenced*. The author believes that the student should be told exactly what is expected of him, and, as soon as he can demonstrate that he can meet this expectation, he should be given credit for it and allowed to move on. His grade should not be determined by the performance of the other students in the class.

When it is possible to meet the objectives at different levels of competence, number grades can be assigned to each level of performance. The author has found that using numbers between 1 and 10 is best suited for this purpose. It is extremely difficult to make the fine discrimination required on a 100-point scale unless a large number of questions or performance items are used.

Now that you and the students know where they are going (objectives) and can determine when they have arrived (criterion tests), you need to find out where your students are now—before they begin working with the modular material.

SUMMARY

Evaluation is an important phase of any teaching/learning process. It is particularly important in modular instruction. The evaluation tools (questions or activities) must measure the competencies outlined in the objectives of the module. The chapter provides a series of guidelines for constructing various types of test items. The differences between "norm-referenced" and "criterion-referenced" evaluation are discussed.

VII

Analysis of Learner Characteristics and Specification of Entry Behavior

---

After reading and studying this chapter, you should be able to:

1. *Analyze a student population with which you are familiar (or a hypothetical one) and describe the general learner characteristics of that population.*
2. *Briefly describe ten learner characteristics which might influence the design of instructional materials.*
3. *Synthesize a sample statement of entry behavior for a module in your subject matter area.*

Designing modular activities begins after you have decided what you want the student to be able to do (objectives). However, before you begin to develop any instructional materials or modules, you *must* be able to describe very precisely the students for whom you are designing the module. You should list in some detail everything you know about the students which might be relevant to their learning the content or skills you hope to teach by means of the module. There are two types of information you will need to specify about your students. The first are general learner characteristics, and the second are statements of entry behavior or what the student is expected to be able to do before he begins the module.

GENERAL LEARNER CHARACTERISTICS

In the process of systematically designing modules, you will need to identify the characteristics of the students for whom you are developing the module. Under the heading of *Learner Characteristics*, you should list any factor that may affect their learning of the materials to be presented. Some of these factors might be:

sex	age/grade level
ethnic origin	socioeconomic background
attention span	emotional maturity
physical or mental handicaps	dexterity for motor tasks
level of motivation	special interests
intelligence	reading ability
visual or audio orientation	technical vocabulary
verbal ability	mathematical ability
learning style	personality characteristics

Note that previous education and experience which relate to the task or subject matter will be discussed later under the heading of *Entry Behavior*.

You need data for each student in order to prescribe a given module for that student. For a module on the western movement during the 1840's in America, the learner characteristics of a specific class might be:

Sixth-grade students, both boys and girls.
Average age: 12 years. Range: 11-14 years.
Middle class, rural socioeconomic background.
No severe physical or mental handicaps.[1]
The attention span ranges from 20 to 30 minutes for most academic tasks.
Less than ten percent of the students are interested in history; thus the motivation level tends to be rather low.
I.Q. ranges from 92 to 126 with seventy-five percent of the students above 100.
The reading ability ranges from 4.2 to 8.6 with eighty percent of the class between 5.5 and 6.5.

In designing a history module for this audience, the developer should keep the time less than twenty minutes if he expects the students to do it in one sitting. It will be necessary to provide motivation. The reading level should be between 5.0 and 6.0. It is important for the developer to keep the learner characteristics in mind as he develops the learning sequence and selects the

---

[1] Usually if none are stated, it is assumed that there are none.

instructional activities and media. Next, we will deal with what the student has already learned or should have learned before he begins the module.

ENTRY BEHAVIOR

Entry behavior is the level of knowledge at which the student begins instruction. Entry behavior includes those abilities which the student already possesses that are relevant to the learning task. This includes the prerequisite knowledge, attitudes or skills which characterize the target population or what you assume the student possesses and may/will require him to demonstrate *before* beginning your module. The purpose of the module is to advance the student from where he is (entry behavior) to where you would like him to be (terminal behavior).

ENTRY BEHAVIORS + MODULE ⟶ TERMINAL BEHAVIORS

Individual modules, although logically related, can be used individually by students or can be combined in several possible sequences. For example, a module on sentence structure might provide the entry behavior for another module on paragraph writing which in turn would be a prerequisite for a module on essays. In a series of modules, the terminal behavior of the first module is often the assumed entry behavior for the second and so forth.

Obviously, it is necessary to clearly specify the skills and knowledge that are needed by the student using the module if he is to succeed. Vague, broad, "shotgun" descriptions lack specificity and are of little or no value to the student because he does not know what is assumed. The teacher designing the module does not know where to begin. And the teacher using the module does not really know whether the module is appropriate for his students. Often, a statement such as "there are no prerequisites for this module" misleads a student into thinking he can succeed when, in reality, he may fail to complete the module satisfactorily because of an insufficient entry behavior. Almost every module will have some prerequisite skills, such as ability to read at a certain level or ability to comprehend spoken language. Another common error is to state in the entry behavior that the student should have "taken a course in welding." He may have taken the course and still not have learned or remember anything about welding.

It is highly recommended that you state the entry behavior in the same format as the objectives. Let's look at a statement of entry behavior for a module on velocity and acceleration with the following general objective:

"Given the description of a physical situation and the necessary data, the student shall be able to calculate the speed, velocity and/or acceleration described. Acceptable performance includes giving both the exact numerical answer and the proper units."

In determining the entry behavior, you ask, "What must the student be able to do before he begins this module?" For the module on velocity and acceleration, the entry behavior would include:

"When given two of the three unknowns, the student should be able to solve simple algebraic manipulations of the following types:

$$x = \frac{y}{z}; \ x = y + z; \ x = y \cdot z; \ and \ x = y - z.\text{"}$$

Of course, you could analyze this statement of entry behavior even further and say, "The student must be able to multiply and divide two digit numbers."

This could be reduced even further: "The student must be able to conduct successive addition and subtraction of two digit numbers."

Carrying this analysis of entry behavior even further, the absurd could be reached for this particular module. For example, "The student must be able to identify numbers between 0 and 100."

List only student capacity and capabilities which have direct relevance to the instructional situation. Factors of accomplishment related indirectly to desired entry behavior can be assumed and need not be spelled out in detail. Referring back to the objective on acceleration, you may assume that, given the necessary equipment, the student could construct with actual apparatus the situation described in the problem. The fact that a student can or cannot drive a car would be irrelevant to this instructional situation even though the principles of speed, velocity and acceleration are incorporated in the operation. Of course, the student must be able to read the instructions. If the module is written at the tenth grade level, the teacher assumes and should test to verify that the student can read at this level with a degree of comprehension specified by the developer.

Normally, entry behavior is analyzed only to the point at which the majority of the students will be able to perform successfully. In the example given previously, the statement about algebraic manipulations is probably as low as is needed in a description of the mathematical component of the entry behavior for the module on speed, velocity and acceleration, since the module is for high school students. A similar analysis of entry behavior would be conducted for the terms which the student should already be able to define and use. For example:

"Given a list of distances, displacements, speeds and velocities, the student should be able to properly identify each. Typical problems would include—3 ft/sec is a____; 6.8 miles northwest is a____; and 8 cm/sec^2 is a____."

Carrying this entry behavior one step lower, you could say,

"Given a number of quantities, the student should be able to state whether each is a scalar or a vector quantity."

In order to carry out this activity, what must the student do?

"The student must be able to define a 'vector' as a quantity which contains both magnitude and direction."

"The student must be able to define 'scalar' as a quantity which has magnitude but no direction."

Going to a still lower level of entry behavior, the student could be required to define and identify "magnitude" and "direction." For twelfth grade students, this would probably be unnecessary. Other relevant entry behavior for this module might be:

"Given a list of fundamental units, the student should be able to classify the units in the proper system (either English or metric)."

"Given a set of measurements, the student should be able to underline the numerical component and circle the unit components."

"Given the prefixes used to denote very small and very large units in the metric system, the student should be able to relate each prefix to the basic unit in the metric system. Typical exercises would include:

2 kilometers = ____ meters and 3 milliseconds = ___ seconds."

The final decision about the necessary entry behavior rests with the instructional developer, and the quality of the analysis is determined by the extent to which the developer knows his students and understands the subject matter.

Unless the necessary entry behavior has been mastered recently, it is advisable to construct and administer a test to measure it. Such a test is an *entry test* which is used to verify that the prerequisites for a given module can be demonstrated by each student before he begins that module. Often, the entry test is combined with the pretest. The distinction between the entry test and the pretest is quite simple. The entry test measures the prerequisites or entry behavior for the module, while the pretest measures the degree of comprehension of the objectives or terminal behavior *before* the student begins the module. The guidelines for constructing entry tests are the same as those for the criterion tests which were discussed in the previous chapter.

SUMMARY

Modules are designed for specific types of students. These students must possess certain characteristics and prerequisite skills in order to benefit fully from the module. A variety of general learner characteristics are described, particularly those which might influence the student's success or failure with the material. Necessary prerequisite skills or entry behavior should also be specified for each module. Since it is impossible to teach everything about a given topic in a short unit of instruction, you must start from a specific point. To be certain that each student has mastered the necessary entry behavior, an entry test may be given.

A module is analogous to a bridge which carries the student from where he is (entry behavior) to where you and hopefully the student would like to be (mastery of the objectives or terminal behavior). Now that the beginning and end points have been determined, let's start building a bridge by looking at the sequencing of instruction and selection of media in the next chapter.

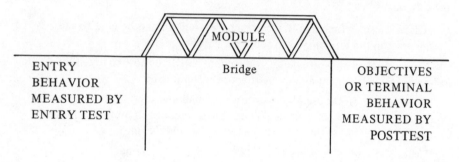

| | Bridge | |
| ENTRY BEHAVIOR MEASURED BY ENTRY TEST | | OBJECTIVES OR TERMINAL BEHAVIOR MEASURED BY POSTTEST |

CHAPTER VIII

Sequencing of Instruction and Selection of Media

After reading and studying this chapter, you should be able to:

1. *Discuss five different techniques for sequencing instruction.*
2. *List and describe four categories of instructional media in·about twenty words each.*
3. *State a rationale and procedure for the selection of media for a module using the media preference hierarchy.*
4. *Analyze any instructional situation and synthesize a recommendation for the media to be used.*
5. *Identify at least five media selection sources (bibliographies).*

After the instructional developer has completed the task analysis, stated the specific performance objectives, designed a criterion test to measure these objectives and described the entry behavior of the students, the next step is arranging the objectives in an order for teaching. The sequence of these objectives will serve as an outline for the module under development.

SEQUENCING OF INSTRUCTION

There is no *one* best way to sequence a particular module. Many times, the sequence is dictated by the subject matter or determined by the characteristics of the students for which the material is being designed. Some sequencing techniques[1] are:

1. Progress from concrete objects or experiences to more abstract ideas.
2. Progress from simple or elementary to more complex manipulations, principles or understandings.
3. Progress from isolated facts to integrated principles or relationships.
4. Progress from specific to general—inductive.
5. Progress from general to specific—deductive.
6. Progress from known to unknown.
7. When teaching a process, progress from beginning to end—temporal or chronological ordering.

At the beginning of the module, you should provide an overview of what the student is going to learn and present the student with the objectives. These give him a goal and eliminate the guesswork about what will be expected of him. Let the student know where he is going and why it is important to go there, i.e., provide a reason for learning. Then, you must design instruction to take him from his entry behavior to the first objective. If the student responds correctly to the first criterion test item within the module, he is ready to move through the material to the second criterion item. If he fails the first criterion item, it is a clue that remedial help is probably needed immediately or that the material should be redesigned. The complete module is designed in this manner—proceeding from one objective to the next until all the objectives have been mastered.

Current educational thinking is that the student should be able to perform as a specialist in the subject matter field would perform. For example, instruction in history is not a matter of teaching or presenting a series of facts and dates but a matter of allowing the student to perform in the way an historian performs. Similarly, a science student should not study *about* science but should *do* science. With this new philosophy for sequencing instruction, content can no longer be considered a series of topics to be presented. Instead, subject matter has become a vehicle for allowing the student to demonstrate and master the behavior called for in the objectives of the module. In order to do this, the student must be actively involved in learning. Often when presented with the objectives and a variety of instructional materials, the student will be able to determine the best sequence for himself and proceed with little or no direction from the teacher.

One technique for sequencing instructional activities is the learning hierarchy as described by Gagné.[2] Each specific skill or objective is placed in a hierarchy in

[1] J. P. DeCecco, *The Psychology of Learning and Instruction: Educational Psychology* (Prentice-Hall: Englewood Cliffs, N.J., 1968), pp. 238-476.

[2] Robert M. Gagné, "Learning and Instructional Sequence" from *Review of Research in Education,* edited by Fred N. Kerlinger (Itasca, Illinois: Peacock Publishers, 1973).

such a way that the skills subordinate to a given skill are hypothesized (and sometimes empirically demonstrated) to contribute substantially to the learning of the given skill. A hierarchy predicts that those students who learn a given skill or objective are most likely to be those who had learned the skills hypothesized as prerequisite to it and least likely to be those who had not learned the prerequisites. Of course, such hierarchies can be tested empirically by trying out the material with students. The critical test of the validity of any learning hierarchy must rest upon the demonstration of transfer of learning to the acquisition of each given skill from those skills hypothesized as being prerequisite to it. No fully satisfactory method of hierarchy validation has been perfected.

Each learning step in the module should be designed to build upon what has come before. Since there are better ways or more efficient and meaningful ways for some students to learn, you should strive to determine and provide the most successful sequence for your students. The success of your sequence will be determined by student tryout. Sequencing is a *means*, not an end. If the students meet the objectives, it works—use it! If not, it has failed—try another! Since there is more than one way to sequence instruction, the instructional developer may want to develop several sequences for the same subject matter and try out each of them to see which works best. Since students differ, you will find that there is no such thing as a single ideal sequence.

SELECTION OF MEDIA

Instructional media can be divided into five basic categories:

1. Printed material
2. Projected media
3. Audio inputs
4. Real objects
5. Human interaction

Printed material includes the textbook, mimeographed instructions, photographs, diagrams, drawings and other references. The projected media are usually 8mm films and 2x2 slides. However, they could include 16mm films, overhead transparencies, filmstrips or videotapes. Audio inputs are usually limited to tape recordings and phonograph records. Real objects cover anything pertinent to the subject matter. Actual materials being discussed or studied should be available to the student whenever possible. The final and probably most important activity is human interaction. This category includes student-teacher and student-student exchange of information. It is vitally important that a teacher be available to answer questions and clarify details not adequately explained in the module for an individual student.

As you select media, you must decide which combination of instructional activities and media will most effectively assist your students in meeting your objectives. It is also important to take into consideration the learner's characteristics, his entry behavior and his needs. The facilities and equipment which are available may limit the types of media which you can use. Your instructional decisions can be tested and the strategies revised on the basis of student tryout.

Most students are highly dependent upon direct experience with materials (real objects, models, diagrams and photographs) for meaningful learning. This is particularly true for the elementary school child. High school and college students have had more experiences with concepts, such as "permeability," "democracy" and "sonnets," so concrete, empirical activity can be reduced and verbal. or didactic instruction increased. However, in modules in which new concepts and terms are introduced, direct experience is usually necessary to facilitate meaningful learning, concept differentiation and generalization.

In the selection of instructional activities and media, it is best to start with real objects or actual experiences whenever possible (see level 1 of the media preference hierarchy—Figure E). Experience is used in the broad sense to include objects, concepts, principles and processes. For example, if you are teaching about bones, the student should actually be able to touch and handle a real bone. However, if you are studying the blue whale, it is impossible to bring a blue whale into the classroom. In this case, you are forced to move to level 2 of the hierarchy and use a model of a blue whale. Sometimes size, cost and danger will prevent the use of real experiences as a part of your module. Many times when the student cannot have real-life experiences (level 1) or be physically involved with an artificial or simulated experience, the student can observe the objects being studied. This approach is used in demonstrations, exhibits and field trips (level 3).

When it is impractical for the student to see actual objects or to have real experiences as learning devices because of the distance, time or number of the objects involved—in many cases just one, i.e., the White House or the Taj Mahal—the designer of instruction is forced to move to the next lower level on the hierarchy and provide indirect perception of the experience by means of television, motion pictures or narrated slides. These media include both the audio and video components. A less desirable but sometimes necessary approach involves just a visual representation of the experience (level 6). The uses of these two types of media are obvious. In some learning situations, the audio representation is superior to the visual presentation, i.e., pronunciation, public speaking and music.

Below these levels are reading about the experience (level 7) and hearing about the experience (level 8). These are the least desirable approaches to instruction but are unfortunately the most frequently used, especially in high school and college.

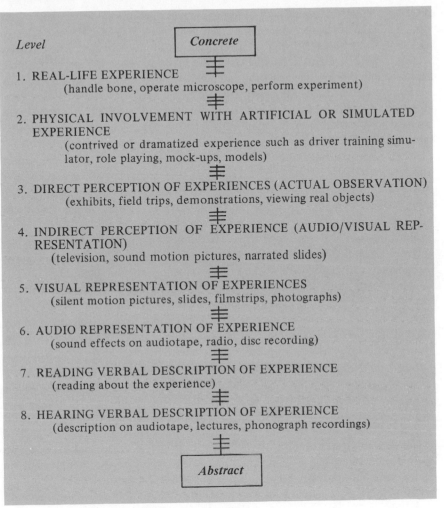

Level

Concrete

1. REAL-LIFE EXPERIENCE
   (handle bone, operate microscope, perform experiment)

2. PHYSICAL INVOLVEMENT WITH ARTIFICIAL OR SIMULATED EXPERIENCE
   (contrived or dramatized experience such as driver training simulator, role playing, mock-ups, models)

3. DIRECT PERCEPTION OF EXPERIENCES (ACTUAL OBSERVATION)
   (exhibits, field trips, demonstrations, viewing real objects)

4. INDIRECT PERCEPTION OF EXPERIENCE (AUDIO/VISUAL REPRESENTATION)
   (television, sound motion pictures, narrated slides)

5. VISUAL REPRESENTATION OF EXPERIENCES
   (silent motion pictures, slides, filmstrips, photographs)

6. AUDIO REPRESENTATION OF EXPERIENCE
   (sound effects on audiotape, radio, disc recording)

7. READING VERBAL DESCRIPTION OF EXPERIENCE
   (reading about the experience)

8. HEARING VERBAL DESCRIPTION OF EXPERIENCE
   (description on audiotape, lectures, phonograph recordings)

Abstract

FIGURE E
Media preference hierarchy.*

*Modified from Edgar Dale's "Cone of Experience." See *Audiovisual Methods in Teaching,* 3rd ed., by Edgar Dale (New York: Holt, Rinehart and Winston, 1969).

Since the activities listed in the figure are a hierarchy, the higher levels (1, 2 and 3) are the most desirable. Generally, it is best to start at level 1 when possible and then move to lower levels only when it is not possible to present material at a higher level. For example, if an elementary teacher is developing a module on farm animals, the ideal form of media according to the media preference hierarchy would be live farm animals which the students could touch and handle. If this is not practical, models of farm animals could be used. Many such toys are commercially available. Another possibility would be a field trip to a farm to look at animals. Moving down the hierarchy, the module could utilize a motion picture or slides of farm animals. An audiotape of barnyard sounds could be used. A lower-level activity would be to have the student read a story about farm animals. Least desirable is the teacher just talking about farm animals. In most modules, a wide variety of different media are used, hence the term multi-media module.

When using any medium, use it to its best advantage. By all means, don't simply lecture on an audiotape. Talk with the students just as you would converse with them in a one-to-one situation. Incorporate simultaneous direct experience by the student into the study material—involve the student! Remember: The student learns by what he does!

Many audio-visual machines, tape recorders and projectors can be readily operated by students, including elementary pupils. However, it may be necessary to include a short teaching or review sequence on the operation of the equipment and procedures to be followed. In many respects, the cassette tape recorder is superior to the more traditional reel-to-reel machine because it is much easier for students to operate. Several machines have a single knob which controls "on-off" and "rewind." A plastic square can be punched out of the back of an audio cassette to prevent the student from accidentally erasing the narration. Most 8mm loop projectors have a single on-off knob and a knob for frame adjustment. Of course, the loop projector avoids the need for rewinding films. Most students experience very little difficulty operating simple recorders and projectors. The student can synchronize an audiotape with an 8mm film so that the normally silent film can be narrated by the instructor.

The use of movies to illustrate a concept or principle shown equally well with a slide or drawing can decrease the cost effectiveness of the module, but, in many cases, motion facilitates understanding. Even if development budgets were unlimited, the time required to design and maintain unnecessary equipment and materials could be better spent in developing additional modules. In reality, money is *always* limited so that every dollar or man-hour spent for superfluous complex equipment or experimentation must be subtracted from the cost effectiveness and/or cost efficiency of the module. The aim of the instructional developer should be to increase student achievement rather than to assemble an impressive display of gadgets.

There is no rule-of-thumb on quality vs. cost decisions for instructional materials. Some instructional aids constructed by the developer may be poor substitutes for materials available commercially which may be purchased at a lower cost, especially when the man-hours required to design and construct an original aid are added to the cost of the material. Consequently, a thorough search of available materials should be conducted after you have determined your objectives and the most appropriate type of media to assist the students in mastering the objectives. An in-depth study of media selection is beyond the scope of this book. However, an annotated list of selection sources follows.

ANNOTATED LIST OF SELECTION SOURCES

General

Guides to Newer Educational Media: Films, Filmstrips, Kinescopes, Phonodiscs, Programmed Instruction Materials, Slides, Transparencies and Video Tapes, published by the American Library Association, 50 East Huron Street, Chicago, Illinois 60611.

An annotated, comprehensive guide which identifies and describes the catalogs, lists, services, professional organizations, journals and periodicals which regularly provide information on educational media.

NICEM (National Information Center for Educational Media). Indexes compiled by the University of Southern California, Los Angeles, California 90007, published by R. R. Bowker (see address under *Books in Print*).

See specific titles under types of media below.

Westinghouse Learning Directory, published by the Westinghouse Learning Corporation, 100 Park Avenue, New York, New York 10017.

A seven-volume list of forty-six different types of media for classroom use in a dictionary arrangement which includes over 600,000 entries under more than 225,000 topic headings as well as source index.

Books

Books in Print, published annually by R. R. Bowker, 1180 Avenue of the Americas, New York, New York 10036.

Author and title indexes to the Publishers Trade List Annual. Includes over 300,000 hardbacks, paperbacks, trade books and textbooks for adults and children, along with a complete publishers' directory.

The Booklist, published by the American Library Association, 50 East Huron Street, Chicago, Illinois 60611.

A journal which is published twice a month and reviews about 125 books, plus pamphlets and audio-visual materials (filmstrips, recordings and films). A good source for information on recent releases.

Films

Film Evaluation Guide, published by the Educational Film Library Association, 17 West Sixtieth Street, New York, New York 10023.

The basic guide provides essential facts about 4500 films and with supplements over 5600 films.

Index to 16mm Educational Films (NICEM)

Contains 70,000 annotated entries to 16mm educational films.

Index to 8mm Motion Cartridges (NICEM)

Contains over 18,000 annotated entries of 8mm cartridges.

Filmstrips

Index to 35mm Filmstrips (NICEM)

Lists and describes 42,000 filmstrips.

Audio

Index to Educational Records (NICEM)

Contains over 18,000 annotated listings of records.

Index to Educational Audio Tapes (NICEM)

Lists and describes over 20,000 audiotapes.

Video Tapes

Index to Educational Video Tapes (NICEM)

Lists and describes over 9000 videotapes.

Overhead Transparencies

Index to Educational Overhead Transparencies (NICEM)

Contains over 35,000 annotated listings of overhead transparencies.

Programmed Instruction

Programmed Learning: A Bibliography of Programs and Presentation Devices, compiled by Carl H. Hendershot, 4114 Ridgewood Drive, Bay City, Michigan 48706.

The loose-leaf format lists over 5000 programs by subject area and by publisher, describes the devices needed in the presentation of programs and cites periodical and text references about programmed instruction.

Supplementary Materials

Free and Inexpensive Learning Materials, compiled and published by George Peabody College for Teachers, Nashville, Tennessee 37203.

Also consult company catalogs, university film catalogs, school district catalogs, teachers and audio-visual specialists.

In some cases, audio-visuals designed by the instructional developer may be better than commercially-prepared ones since the latter may contain information and detail which is not relevant to the specific objectives of the module. It is important to keep diagrams and models simple. Complex diagrams, unnecessarily long films or slide sequences and complicated models or printed materials tend to confuse rather than to clarify. Irrelevant details distract from learning! The developer must search continually for the most efficient way to meet the objectives at the lowest total cost per student.

Many times, the instructional materials can be taken to the object or area being studied. For example, a tape recorder and a text can be taken to a museum, or a tape and a series of slides can be taken by a student-operator to the shop and studied while learning to use large, immovable pieces of equipment.

SUMMARY

After you have decided what you are going to teach (objectives) and in what order (sequence), then you must decide how you are going to teach it (instructional activities and media). There are a number of approaches for sequencing instructional activities, such as concrete to abstract, general to specific and chronological. The one to use is determined by the nature of the subject matter and the type of students. The appropriateness of the sequence can be tested by student tryout as described in the next chapter.

The types of media used can be classified as printed materials, projected media, audio, real objects and human interaction. An annotated list of selection sources is included in this chapter. When selecting media, "Don't get the cart before the horse!" Don't select the specific medium until you have carefully examined the various possibilities using the Media Preference Hierarchy and start with the most concrete when possible.

CHAPTER IX

Student Tryout of the Module

After reading and studying this chapter, you should be able to:

1. *Discuss the rationale for student tryout of modules. Your discussion should include the purposes of student tryout.*
2. *List and describe three types of feedback (indicators) which can be used to assess the effectiveness of the module.*
3. *Justify the statement, "Don't finalize your module too early! Wait until after student tryout." Your justification should include the reasons for not finalizing your module before student tryout and three techniques which can be used to avoid premature finalization of the module.*
4. *Briefly describe the type of student who should be used for student tryout.*
5. *Analyze the student attitudes which must be dealt with before student tryout and synthesize a procedure for doing so. Your discussion should address itself to the following: student test anxiety, aversion to criticism and dislike for self-instruction (if appropriate).*
6. *Describe three techniques for student tryout of modules in each of the following formats: a. self-instructional, b. small group and c. large group.*
7. *Outline a procedure for conducting a student tryout.*
8. *Conduct a student tryout of your module and prepare a student tryout evaluation sheet.*

The success of your module is determined largely by the amount of time and effort you devote to trying it out with real, live students. The purpose of student tryout is to improve the material. As the students concentrate on the material, the developer evaluates the effectiveness of the module by observing the students' behavior. Ultimately, the purpose of student tryout is to meet the objectives of the module and at the same time to make the material neither so easy that it bores the students nor so difficult that it frustrates them.

The most objective means of improving the module from student tryout is an examination of the errors in the students' responses to questions contained within the module and on criterion items, such as the posttest. In addition, observable student behavior such as chewing his pencil, cursing the material under his breath or appearing uninterested can provide valuable feedback to the alert instructional developer. Spoken comments (such as "Gee! This is kid's stuff" or "I can't dig this") indicate the student's impression of the material. While conducting your tryouts be on the lookout for all three types of these valuable indicators—written responses (answers to questions in the material), non-verbal behaviors (gestures) and spoken comments. A checklist and comment sheet (see page 81) may aid the teacher in recording the student responses to the module. If the student is given any paper-and-pencil exercises, include them with your evaluation. The student tryout evaluation sheets can be summarized and the results can be used to make the necessary revisions in the module.

On the basis of student reaction and response to the material, the instructional developer revises the module. The only way to be certain that the revisions have been beneficial is to test the revised material with other students. Thus, the student tryout cycle becomes: design, test, revise, test . . . revise, test. Note that you should always end the cycle with a test to make certain that the material is still effective. There is no magic or sacred number of tests that should be conducted. Needless to say, it depends to a great extent on the ability of the developer to know his audience, to understand his material and to communicate it to his students via the module.

The format of the module for student tryout depends upon the individual developer, the context of the subject matter and the objectives. Usually, it is best to keep the material in a rough form. If you plan to use a series of slides made from pictures in a book, you might use the original pictures with a few students before you go to the trouble and expense of making the slides and having them developed. You might also get by with a rough audiotape or with just reciting the material to be taped rather than actually recording it for the early tryouts. It has been found that if a developer spends a lot of time and energy producing a professional product before student tryout, he is usually very reluctant to change or modify the materials even though the student tryout dictates it. The moral—don't finalize your module too early! Wait until after the student tryout.

Name _____ Date _____

A. Answers to Questions within Module

                                                     Correct   Incorrect

    1. _____

    2. _____

    3. _____

    4. _____

    5. _____

    6. _____

                  .

                  .

                  .

              etc.

          Posttest Results   _____

B. Non-Verbal Behaviors and Gestures

C. Student Comments about Subject Matter or Module

FIGURE F
Student tryout evaluation sheet.

For example, rather than going to the trouble of preparing detailed drawings, be satisfied with rough sketches until you have tried them out with students. It is best to keep the study guide and any other handouts in small, manageable pieces. The reasons—it is much easier to retype the material if you need to revise just a paragraph or two, and it is much easier to rearrange or re-sequence your instructions when they can easily be broken apart. You may find also that you need to add material or that you wish to delete some extraneous information. These operations are easily facilitated by having the information divided into small, manageable pieces.

If you plan to use an audiotape but do not want to record the information on a tape during early stages of student tryout, you can put the instructions on cards and read the material to the students. Then, when revision is necessary, you can rearrange or revise the cards before the next tryout.

Depending upon the nature of your module, you may or may not want to include the correct answers to questions included in your material during student tryout. One alternative would be to ask the student to write down his answer and confirm it by saying, "That's right!" Many of these original student responses can be used later as models or as the correct responses in the final version of the material.

There are at least three advantages to the instructional developer testing the material himself during the student tryout. First, he becomes aware of his own weaknesses as an instructional developer. He also receives the maximum possible feedback from the situation; sometimes it can be very ego deflating but other times very rewarding. Finally, he can revise the faulty material during the student tryout and avoid student frustration if the original material is faulty.

Every module should be designed for a specific audience. Obviously, the student for the tryout should come from this audience. The student should have the entry behavior (prerequisites) and not have the terminal behavior. Otherwise, the success or failure of the module cannot be adequately judged from the student's performance. The first group of students used for tryout should be highly communicative. Later, you should use students from the full range of the intended population.

In order to increase the effectiveness of the student tryout, several student attitudes must be taken into consideration. Test anxiety must be reduced. If the instructional material contains questions and performance situations, the student may regard it as a test and be anxious or afraid of making errors while responding. Most students hesitate to criticize the teacher or materials developed by the teacher. Therefore, it is important to establish the proper conditions before the student begins the module. In your instructions or introduction of the material to the students, you might include some of the following ideas:

A. Reduce the students' test anxiety—

"I want to test this material, not you. Your errors will help me locate portions of the material which need improvement."

B. Reduce the aversion to criticism—

"This is some material which has been developed by a group of people.

They are asking you to help them locate errors, difficulties and weak spots in it."

C. Reduce the students' dislike for self-instruction if the module is designed to be self-instructional—

"Since I am trying to determine the self-sufficiency of the material, you should ask me for help only after giving the material a very careful reading."

Explicit instructions on how to go through the material and how to operate any of the necessary equipment should always be included.

It is helpful to alert the student to the types of questions you plan to ask him upon his completion of the module. Here are some possible questions:

"Did you find any place where the material was dull or boring? Show or tell me where."

"Are you still not sure about any of the ideas or concepts presented in the module?"

"Do you have any specific comments or suggestions for improving this module so it would be more meaningful for other students?"

"Was there any place in the material where you thought there was a gap or a sudden jump from one topic or procedure to another?"

"Was there any place where you had difficulty?"

"Did you enjoy this module?"

The way you react to the students' mistakes, hesitations and criticisms during the tryout will affect the validity and quantity of the feedback which you receive during the student tryout.

SELF-INSTRUCTIONAL

The way in which you conduct the student tryout will depend upon the type of module, i.e., 1. self-instructional, 2. small group or 3. class (large group). Since many modules are of the first type—self-instructional, let's look at some of the techniques which will facilitate student tryout of this type of module. Even though you are present during student tryout of self-instructional materials, you must be careful not to give unnecessary, additional assistance. The instructional developer can unconsciously help the student with subtle clues. For example, you might read a question for the student with an emphasis on the key word or underline the important word or sentence in the material while the student is reading it. Of course, underlining key words is okay if the underline is going to be a revision of the material. Some observers change their expression whenever the student is about to make a "mistake." As a result of these and similar clues, the effectiveness of the material in actual, individual use later may differ radically from its apparent effectiveness during student tryout.

The developer must have some way to note his comments and possible revisions during the student tryout. He may use a blank sheet of paper, a student tryout evaluation sheet or a duplicate copy of the materials. The developer should make pertinent notations on his copy to help him make the revisions later. The most useful type of note taking is to indicate the suggested revision on the duplicate copy of the material.

When a student hesitates over a portion of the module, the developer faces two related problems. One, rushing to the student's aid too quickly and not giving the material a chance to prove its effectiveness may increase the student's aversion to self-instruction. Two, not helping him at all might frustrate the student to the extent that he loses interest in the testing session. If the student hesitates for a long time over one portion of material or if he gives an unusual and incorrect response to a question (assuming that you are not able to guess what is wrong with the material or the question), you should ask the student how he arrived at the answer.

If the developer keeps on revising his material during and after each student tryout, he should find the number of necessary revisions decreasing, unexpected reaction from the students decreasing and errors on specific questions decreasing.

SMALL GROUP

If the module involves a small group discussion, the developer should make an audiotape of the discussion, particularly if he is also a participant or coordinator in the discussion. As the developer, you should only assume the role which you or another teacher will assume with the final format of the module. Don't apologize for the material and by all means don't give additional, detailed explanation of the content unless the explanation will be part of the module in its final form.

If you are just an observer during the tryout, you can note the nature of the interaction which takes place between the students or between the students and the media. In addition to noting or collecting the students' written responses to questions and exercises during the instruction, you will probably want to conduct a debriefing with the students after the tryout has been completed. You may also want to ask the students to provide a written evaluation of the module in addition to taking the posttest.

LARGE GROUP

Some modules may involve a presentation to a large group of students (thirty or more). The presentation may be mediated (i.e., a film or slide-tape program) or a live lecture. If it is a live presentation, a videotape of the lecture will allow you to analyze it in detail later.

As in the other types of modules, use a rough format of the materials. For example, if the final form of the presentation will include a 16mm film, you can use a videotape for the student tryout since the videotape is less expensive to produce, the results are immediate (no developing time as with film) and the videotape can be revised more easily.

After the modules have been tried out with a group of students, solicit their comments either in a written or oral format. If the group size is large, a computer scored evaluation form may be the most efficient way to obtain the necessary information with which to revise the module. Such a form is described in Chapter X. When you are satisfied with the module and do not feel that additional tryout will be beneficial, it is time to move to the final phase of instructional development—evaluation, which is the topic of Chapter X.

SUMMARY

A very important step in the development of modular instruction is the actual tryout of the material with students. The module is tested and revised until most of the students master the objectives. If the students do not achieve, the module has failed and must be revised.

During student tryout the module should be in a rough draft format so it can be revised easily. It is important to properly prepare the students for the tryout by reducing their test anxiety and aversion to criticizing. You may also alert them to the type of information you are seeking as a result of the tryout.

CHAPTER X

Evaluation
of the Module

After reading and studying this chapter, you should be able to:

1. *State and explain the basic questions to be answered during modular evaluation. Your explanation should include the four basic types of information to be collected.*
2. *Distinguish between "effectiveness" and "efficiency" in relation to the evaluation of a module.*
3. *Given evaluation data for a module, calculate correctly the effectiveness and/or efficiency of the module.*

The purpose of evaluation is to enable one to measure and predict the success of a module. The basic question to be asked is:

"WHO learns WHAT under WHICH CONDITIONS
and in HOW MUCH TIME?"

Your evaluation should collect the following information:

WHO is the target population of the module? The answer to this question will be a description of the student population upon which you tested your module, including the number of students, their ages, grade level, the range of reading abilities, I.Q.'s, previous achievement and other relevant background information. If a module is designated for a certain age or grade level, it does *not* necessarily follow that everyone of that age or at that grade level will benefit from it.

WHAT does the module teach? The answer to this question will be a measure of the extent to which the objectives are met by the students. The answer may be a comparison of the pretest and posttest results, written exercises or products of a number of students who have completed the module.

Under WHICH CONDITIONS does the module function best? The answer to this question pertains to how the module should be administered. Does it require a learning laboratory with elaborate displays? Is it designed to have an instructor present when the student is going through it? What are the scheduling requirements? Can the student do it at home or in the library? Does the module require supplementary or adjunct materials? A thorough description of the test situation should be included with your evaluation.

Each of the statements below expresses a feeling toward biology. Please rate each statement on the extent to which you agree. For each, you may: (A) Strongly Agree, (B) Agree, (C) Be Undecided, (D) Disagree or (E) Strongly Disagree.

After you have made your choice, blacken in the appropriate response in the columns on the IBM card corresponding to each item.

A	B	C	D	E
Strongly Agree	Agree	Undecided	Disagree	Strongly Disagree

1. Biology is very interesting to me.
2. I *don't* like biology, and it scares me to have to take it.
3. I am always under a terrible strain in a biology class.
4. Biology is fascinating and fun.
5. Biology makes me feel secure, and at the same time it is stimulating.
6. Biology makes me feel uncomfortable, restless, irritable and impatient.
7. In general, I have a good feeling toward biology.
8. When I hear the word biology, I have a feeling of dislike. ·
9. I approach biology with a feeling of hesitation.
10. I really like biology.
11. I have always enjoyed studying biology in school.
12. It makes me nervous to even think about doing a biology experiment.
13. I feel at ease in biology and like it very much.
14. I feel a definite positive reaction to biology; it's enjoyable.

FIGURE G
Biology attitude scale.

Developed under National Science Foundation Grant #GY7664 to the Minicourse Development Project at Purdue University. Copyright © 1972, Purdue Research Foundation.

Below are some scales on which we would like you to rate your feelings toward biology. On each scale, you can rate your feelings toward biology as A, B, C, D or E. THERE ARE NO CORRECT ANSWERS. Also, some of the scales seem to make more sense than others. Don't worry about it. Just rate your feelings toward biology on these scales as best you can. Please don't leave any scales blank.

For your response to each scale, blacken in the appropriate box on the IBM card.

BIOLOGY IS:

15.	Good	A	B	C	D	E	Bad
16.	Clean	A	B	C	D	E	Dirty
17.	Worthless	A	B	C	D	E	Valuable
18.	Cruel	A	B	C	D	E	Kind
19.	Pleasant	A	B	C	D	E	Unpleasant
20.	Sad	A	B	C	D	E	Happy
21.	Nice	A	B	C	D	E	Awful
22.	Fair	A	B	C	D	E	Unfair

FIGURE G (Continued)

The TIME requirement is also an important factor. How long will it take a student to successfully complete the module? The answer to this question should include the time ranges, as well as the mean, median and mode times. This information is very important for scheduling considerations, as well as for efficiency determinations. Perhaps the teacher or a traditional text could achieve the same objectives in less time, at a lower cost and therefore function more efficiently than the module.

You may also be concerned about any changes in the students' attitudes toward the subject matter. It is possible to teach the material to the student (gain in achievement) and at the same time teach them to dislike the subject (more negative attitudes). An example of an attitude scale is shown in Figure G on pages 88 and 89. A scale such as this may not detect changes in attitude as the result of a single module; in fact, there may be no significant change in attitude due to one module. However, you can measure changes in attitude, if they exist, over a semester or a school year.

You may also be interested in the students' reaction to the module. Were the objectives clearly stated? Was it stimulating? You can ask a few students for their opinions. However, when you are evaluating your module with a large number of students, you may want to use a form which can be rapidly scored and interpreted. The Minicourse Development Project at Purdue University has developed a twenty-one-item evaluation form which can be computer scored.

Minicourse Evaluation

Evaluator:

Minicourse development is a long and often painstaking process. The minicourse that you have just completed has undergone several modifications and refinements, primarily directed by the constructive criticism of students in the past. As an integral part of our program of minicourse development, YOUR help is needed.

Please read each item carefully and choose the answer (A, B, C, D or E) that comes *closest* to your feelings on the matter. When you have made your choice, darken in the appropriate bracket for the corresponding item ON THE COMPUTER CARD. DO NOT write on the questionnaire itself. Also, since we are only interested in your FRANK evaluation of the minicourse, please DO NOT write your name on the computer card but please DO be honest in your evaluation. Indicate the title of the minicourse on the TOP of the computer card.

Finally, a separate COMMENT SHEET is provided for any additional comments, criticisms and suggestions you may care to make with respect to the minicourse. Your cooperation is appreciated.

Below are two example items. The first item contains a standardized rating scale with five anchor points: Strongly Agree (SA); Agree (A); Neither Agree, Nor Disagree (N); Disagree (D); Strongly Disagree (SD).

Example A:

	SA	A	N	D	SD
The United States is in need of a National Health Program. (If you neither agree nor disagree, blacken in column C on the IBM card).	A	B	C	D	E

The second type of item on the questionnaire contains an open-ended statement to which you will be required to respond more specifically.

Example B:

Current progress in developing a National Health Program has been

A	B	C	D	E
Too slow		About right		Too fast

(If your feelings more closely correspond to about right, blacken in column C on the IBM card.)

OBJECTIVES	SA	A	N	D	SD
1. The objectives were very clearly stated.	A	B	C	D	E

FIGURE H

Purdue Minicourse evaluation questionnaire.

Designed and developed under National Science Foundation Grant #GY7664 to the Minicourse Development Project at Purdue University. Copyright © 1972, Purdue Research Foundation.

	SA	A	N	D	SD
2. The materials presented were related to the objectives.	A	B	C	D	E
3. I feel that the stated objectives for this minicourse were achieved.	A	B	C	D	E

AUDIO

	SA	A	N	D	SD
4. Voice quality was very clear.	A	B	C	D	E
5. Speaker's mood was very enthusiastic.	A	B	C	D	E
6. Instructions were clear and easy to follow.	A	B	C	D	E
7. Instructions for the exercises/activities were adequately explained for my knowledge of the topic.	A	B	C	D	E

8. Pacing

A	B	C	D	E
Too slow		About right		Too fast

9. Overall evaluation of audio presentation

A	B	C	D	E
Excellent	Good	Average	Below Aver.	Poor

STUDY GUIDE AND HANDOUTS

	SA	A	N	D	SD
10. The written material was clearly presented.	A	B	C	D	E
11. The written material was brief and to the point.	A	B	C	D	E
12. The study guide and audio tape were very well synchronized.	A	B	C	D	E

VISUALS (photos, charts and diagrams)
Note: If there were no visuals in this minicourse, leave questions 13-15 blank.

13. In general, the visuals were of excellent quality (clarity).	A	B	C	D	E
14. The visuals were smoothly presented and integrated within the sequence of the minicourse.	A	B	C	D	E
15. The visuals were *effective* in contributing to my understanding of the subject matter.	A	B	C	D	E

TANGIBLES (specimens and models)
Note: If there were no tangibles in this minicourse, leave questions 16-17 blank.

16. In general, the tangibles were smoothly presented and integrated within the sequence of the minicourse.	A	B	C	D	E

FIGURE H (Continued)

		SA	A	N	D	SD
17.	The tangibles were *effective* in contributing to my understanding of the subject matter.	A	B	C	D	E

GENERAL

		SA	A	N	D	SD
18.	I found this minicourse very stimulating.	A	B	C	D	E
19.	This minicourse was very organized.	A	B	C	D	E
20.	This minicourse was relevant to my interests.	A	B	C	D	E
21.	I spent approximately_____on this minicourse.	A	B	C	D	E

A	B	C	D	E
Less than an hour	1 hour	1½ hours	2 hours	More than 2 hours

Please make any additional comments, criticisms and suggestions relevant to this minicourse on the COMMENT SHEET.

Thanks again for your cooperation!

FIGURE H (Continued)

This questionnaire is shown in Figure H on pages 90-92. You will probably need to adapt the form to your individual needs and the specifics of your module.

There are two other types of evaluation which will be discussed—effectiveness and efficiency. *Effectiveness* is a measure of student achievement. In other words, what has the student gained from studying the module? *Efficiency* is a measure of the achievement per unit time. Two modules could meet the same objectives, but, if one module does it in half the time, it is twice as efficient even though the effectiveness is the same. Another factor in efficiency may be cost or the consideration of the achievement per dollar spent per student.

Usually, a representative group of students completes the module under controlled conditions to provide data about the effectiveness and/or efficiency of the instructional system. In order to calculate the efficiency of a module, one needs to measure the entry behavior (performance) of the student, the terminal behavior (performance) of the student and the time needed to complete the module. The following formulas are then used:

$$\text{Effectiveness} = \text{Terminal Behavior} - \text{Entry Behavior}$$
$$\text{Efficiency} = \frac{\text{Effectiveness}}{\text{Time}} = \frac{\text{Terminal} - \text{Entry Behavior}}{\text{Time}}$$

To illustrate the use of these formulas, let's assume the following group data have been collected:

"A group of twenty students correctly responded to an average of twenty percent of the items on the pretest. After spending an average of sixty minutes studying the module, they scored ninety-five percent on the posttest."

Under the above conditions, the effectiveness was:

$$\text{Effectiveness} = 95\% - 20\% = 75\% \text{ increase}$$

While the efficiency was:

$$\text{Efficiency} = \frac{95\% - 20\%}{60 \text{ min.}} = \frac{75\%}{60 \text{ min.}} = 1.25\%/\text{min.}$$

Experienced instructional developers find it more useful to compute the achievement for each student separately. Thus, the effectiveness and/or efficiency is calculated for each student, then the data are pooled and the final results tabulated. An alternative method for calculating effectiveness for an individual student is the *Modified Gain Score*. It has the advantage of taking into account the total possible achievement or maximum possible score on the test.

$$\text{Gain Score* } = \text{Terminal Behavior} - \text{Entry Behavior}$$

$$\text{Modified Gain Score } = \frac{\text{Terminal} - \text{Entry Behavior}}{\text{Maximum Possible} - \text{Entry Behavior}}$$

For an individual student who scored ten percent on the pretest and ninety percent on the posttest, the gain score would be calculated as follows:

$$\text{Gain Score } = 90\% - 10\% = 80\%$$

The Modified Gain Score would be:

$$\text{Modified Gain Score } = \frac{90\% - 10\%}{100\% - 10\%} = \frac{80\%}{90\%} = .888$$

For groups of students, the *Mean Modified Gain Score* is usually represented. The Mean Modified Gain Score is simply the average of the Modified Gain Scores for each student. An alternative calculation would be to use the average pretest and posttest scores in the above formula. For the group data above, the Mean Modified Gain Score would be:

$$\text{Mean Modified Gain Score} = \frac{95\% - 20\%}{100\% - 20\%} = \frac{75\%}{80\%} = .9375$$

The Modified Gain Score takes into account the maximum possible gain as compared to the actual gain. It is possible to have two modules with the same actual gain but different Modified Gain Scores.

*Called effectiveness earlier in the chapter.

Module A		*Module B*	
Entry Test	20%	Entry Test	60%
Posttest	60%	Posttest	100%
Gain Score	40%	Gain Score	40%
Modified Gain Score =		Modified Gain Score =	

$$\frac{60\% - 20\%}{100\% - 20\%} = \frac{40\%}{80\%} = .500 \qquad \frac{100\% - 60\%}{100\% - 60\%} = \frac{40\%}{40\%} = 1.000$$

In addition to calculating efficiency, it is important to know the time needed to complete the module and the total cost per student. A teacher will need to know how much time to include in the class schedule for the students to go through the module. Will most of the students complete the module in a class period (approximately forty-five minutes)? The teacher will need to plan additional activities for elementary or secondary students if there are significant time differences between early finishers and late finishers. Assuming that the teacher has been meeting the same objectives in two hours of class time, will the module save time and thus be more efficient than his usual approach? In order to answer these questions, you will need to know the mean time, the median time and the range of time usually required to satisfactorily complete the module and meet the objectives.

Another important concern for educators today is economy. How much will it cost per student to complete the module? How does this cost compare with the current costs for your instruction? Even though the initial expenditure for equipment and facilities may be high, the largest cost is usually the expense of designing and developing the instructional materials.

SUMMARY

Evaluation of modular instruction should answer the question"WHO learns WHAT under WHICH CONDITIONS and in HOW MUCH TIME?" Of utmost concern is the effectiveness and/or efficiency of a given module. The preceding chapters have described in detail the design, development and evaluation of modules. Now, let's turn our attention to the utilization of modules in actual teaching situations.

CHAPTER XI

The Utilization
of Modules

After reading and studying this chapter, you should be able to:

1. *Describe how modular instruction can be used for each of the following:*
   a. *Regular instruction*
   b. *Enrichment*
   c. *Remedial instruction*
   d. *Establishing entry behavior*
   e. *Absentee instruction*
   f. *Correspondence courses*
2. *Synthesize a situation in your field in which modular instruction could be used effectively. Your description should include the type of objectives to be achieved, the characteristics and entry behavior of the student, the role of the teacher, the types of media and instructional activities to be used and the format of the module (individual, small group or large group).*

What are some of the many uses of modules in instruction? Because modules are so broad in their application and can incorporate a variety of media and instructional activities, they can literally be used to teach *anybody anything!* Of course, their most popular use to date has been and probably will continue to be academic instruction in elementary schools, high schools, colleges and universities. However, modules can be used for non-academic instruction. Included in this application are self-improvement (such as, "Increase Your Vocabulary" and "Ten Steps to Improve Physical Fitness"), hobbies and crafts (with topics such as "How to Play Chess" and "Macramé Made Simple") and travel and recreation (for example, "A Walking Tour of the Smithsonian Institution" and "Fly Casting").

The more common uses of modules include regular instruction, enrichment, remedial instruction, establishing entry behavior, absentee instruction and correspondence courses.

REGULAR INSTRUCTION

Modules can be used to teach part of a course, all of a course or a total curriculum. In a conventional high school biology course, a module such as *Mimicry* could be used to teach a portion of the content. With a few minor modifications such as substituting color slides for the specimens, the module could be converted from individual to group use. The film loop which accompanies *Mimicry* is suitable for either small group or individual use.

A modular system is used for teaching all of a high school biology course at West Lafayette (Indiana) High School.[1] The West Lafayette biology program provides several options for the students who are mostly ninth graders. Based upon the premise that all students do not learn effectively in the same manner, at least five options are provided for them.

1. They may use modules with an audiotape developed by the instructor.
2. They may use modules with a transcript of the audiotape.
3. They may read a textbook. Specific page numbers are given for each performance objective.
4. They may use another student as a performance instructor.
5. They may use the teacher as a resource person and tutor.

Actually, most students use a combination which may prove most satisfactory to them as individuals. The West Lafayette system recognizes that there is no one best way and allows the student a chance to develop his own style of learning and his own pattern of study.

Inquiry activities and value training are integrated into the biology course at West Lafayette High School. Students discuss their values and beliefs concerning

---

[1] Information provided by Ken Bush, Biology Department Chairman, Dave McGaw and Curt Smiley, instructors. See also "Audio-Tutorial Learning in the Secondary School," by D. H. McGaw, C. A. McGaw, K. H. Bush, R. N. Hurst, and C. L. Smiley in *Individualized Science Like It Is,* edited by Henry J. Triezenberg (National Science Teachers Association, 1972).

topics in the course. For example, when studying the effect of nicotine on cells, the students are asked to consider the question of whether or not they are going to smoke. The students form a value system of their own which relates to the factual materials under study in the module. When possible, the information presented in the modules is related to everyday problems. The students are also encouraged to get together and design experiments which will help them apply the knowledge they gain from the factual part of the modules.

One of the most important aspects of using modular instruction is the overall instructional system in which the modules are used. Each teacher must devise his own system for his particular situation. Let's look at the West Lafayette biology system, *A Systems Approach to Biology*. At West Lafayette, they use an activities flow chart which is shown in Figure H. The flow chart is a guide to the sequencing of student activities and responsibility. There are eight components in the West Lafayette system. The first component is the statement of performance objectives. Objectives were discussed in detail in Chapter IV of this text. Sample objectives from a West Lafayette module are shown on page 104. The next component is the individual module itself. The study guide for a module on photosyntheses is reproduced on pages 104-107. The modules involve a variety of instructional activities and media. This is the stage where most of the cognitive learning takes place. In the modules, students listen to tapes, read, observe demonstrations, interpret data and in general obtain the necessary background to analyze and investigate in later phases of the course.

If after working with the modular materials the student feels confident with the stated objectives, he is ready to proceed to the third component of the system, called the "TRIP." Most people would refer to this activity as a test. "TRIP" is a short for "Testing Regular Instructional Performance." Each student takes an oral and a written quiz on each module. Orals are taken in groups of three to eight students with an interchange of discussion and are evaluated by the instructor. The writtens are taken individually, and the student must correctly respond to eighty percent of the questions. Mastery on the oral and written earns a grade of "C" on that particular lesson or module. A student must complete this much on all modules during the year to earn a grade of "C" for the course. In other words, a student would only have to do steps 1, 2 and 3 on every lesson in order to earn a grade of "C" for the course.

Component 4 is called *Performance Instruction* and is an optional step. A student can receive performance instruction or tutorial help from a peer if he so desires. However, it is not a required step. If a student does not understand part or all of a module, he may ask any student who has satisfactorily completed the "TRIP" or test for that particular module to help him. The student needing help gets it immediately and does not have to wait for the regular instructor. At the same time, the student serving as a performance instructor has his own learning reinforced. A familiar adage is: "You don't really know something until you can

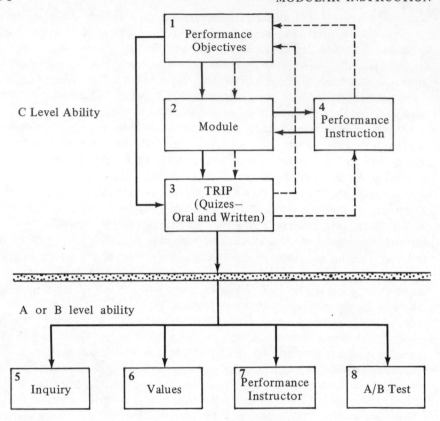

—————————Possible pathways toward a successful A, B or C grade.

— — — — — —Possible pathways if student is unsuccessful on his quiz attempt.

FIGURE I
Activities flow chart.

From K. L. Bush, David H. McGaw, and Curtis L. Smiley, *Systems Approach to Biology Energy Study Guide*. West Lafayette, Indiana: Diversified Educational Enterprises Incorporated, 1971.

teach it to somebody else." The most important contribution of this component to the instructional system is that there are several instructors per classroom instead of only one.

How can a student earn a grade of "A" or "B" in the course? Basically, he does this by earning bonus points. There are four means of earning additional points for an A or B grade. These are identified on the flow chart in Figure I as components 5, 6, 7 and 8. One method of earning points is by doing inquiries. Inquiries are activities which most students enjoy. They involve investigations listed in the study guides (see page 107, from laboratory manuals or student designed investigations on the topics of particular interest. Inquiries are chosen from a group available for each module and may be completed individually or in small groups. Inquiries are usually conducted in the laboratory. Group meetings are then held to discuss several areas of investigation such as variables, control, sources of error, interpretation of data and any other pertinent points that arise as a result of the investigation. A write-up is required for each investigation. Up to ten points may be recorded for every inquiry completed.

Component 6 is the value phase. This phase incorporates what may be one of the most interesting features of the West Lafayette system. The value activities require students to do some independent library research in order to take a position on a debatable question currently pertinent to society (see page 108). Students discuss the question posed during arranged meetings. The teacher tries not to take an active part or play much of a role except to moderate. However, these discussions become so stimulating that sometimes it is difficult for the teacher to stay out of them! Following the discussion meeting, each student must write a position paper justifying the position he took. There is not a right or wrong answer for this activity. The purpose of the value activity is to develop processes and skills for the students to use in all aspects of life, not just biology or science. Up to ten points can be awarded for each value completed, and these are credited toward the A or B grade.

By serving as a performance instructor as described above a student may earn A or B points. He may receive points as a performance instructor only once for each module, and he only receives credit if the student he has helped satisfactorily completes the TRIP on the module. Each performance instructor rating is worth ten points. Actually, most students are willing to help more than one student if they are asked to do so, even though they receive the bonus points only once.

One other way to earn A or B points is by taking an A/B test as shown by component 8 in the flow chart. The A/B tests are forty point tests. There are forty items, each item worth one point. There is only one A/B test for each unit (which is composed of three to six modules), and it is administered only once at the end of the unit. The A/B tests are not graded A, B, C, etc., but the number of points earned is credited toward a student's A or B grade. The A/B test is a difficult test which has been designed to measure higher levels of learning and achievement than the TRIP test.

From these four available ways of obtaining A/B points, the student may choose any combination he desires. Some students avoid the A/B tests, a few dislike inquiry, and others don't care for values, and there are a few who don't want to take the time to help another student. However, each student is competing against himself, not other students.

The biology teachers in the West Lafayette modular system feel their time is much more efficiently and effectively used. They also feel the students' time is much more efficiently and effectively used in the modular system than in the conventional system in which the students sit in classrooms and listen to teachers. The students appreciate knowing what is expected of them and where they are going by the use of performance objectives.

The modular program at West Lafayette is based upon five principles.

1. Make the Best Use of the Instructor's Time.

The West Lafayette biology teachers found upon examination of their teaching that they did not always make the best use of their instruction time, but that, if given a chance, the students could decide how best to use the instructor's time. When the students come to an instructor, they make the best use of his time. By utilizing modules, a significant portion of the teacher's time during the day is available to the students, and there are ways for the students to get additional help in learning.

2. Make the Best Use of the Student's Time.

In the West Lafayette biology course, most of the factual information and directions are on audiotapes. The audiotapes are used in the carrels in the learning center. The student is *self-paced*; he can go over the information and materials as many times as he wishes or he can turn the information off if he wants to. The students can replay, relisten, turn off and do things at their convenience. The student himself is in the best position to make the wisest use of his own time—this is referred to as "self-pacing."

If the student has a problem, he can go to the instructor for immediate help. The teachers are available when the students need help. Making the best use of student's time is very important, although there must be some reasonable deadline to help the students make steady progress.

3. Performance Objectives Are Absolutely Essential.

Performance objectives are important to the teachers and to the students because they define precisely what the students are expected to do. As the teachers examined their teaching closely, they realized that much of their teaching prior to using performance objectives must have been very frustrating to their students. The teachers were ambiguous many times, and they over generalized, and they were unaware of the problems that they were causing their students. They have found since that performance objectives are effective in alleviating the problems in the original teaching situation.

4. Students Are Good Teachers.

Peer instruction is an integral part of the system. Students often study and work together in pairs or teams. In addition to performance instruction (component 4 on the activities flow chart) which was described earlier, students help each other to master the objectives since the criteria for achievement are fixed and there is no competition among students for grades as there would be using the normal curve.

5. Mastery of Subject Matter Is Necessary.

Students take both written and oral quizzes after completing each module and are expected to master the lesson to the specified criterion. On the oral, a student is given a performance objective at random from the list for that module, and he must respond to that performance objective. The purpose of the oral is to have the student communicate his knowledge of that particular performance objective. If he demonstrates competence with the objective, he earns completion for that part of the evaluation. For the written part of the examination on the module, the student is required to achieve eighty percent on the written questions to obtain completion. The minimum requirements have been carefully defined, and the student must master the material before going on. He may retake oral or written examinations as often as is necessary before going on. The instructors maintain continuous records of each student's progress. The instructors feel that mastery may well be the most important principle in the West Lafayette modular system.

Evidence indicates that there is higher achievement by the students using the mastery approach compared to students using a traditional approach.[2] The West Lafayette biology students exceed the national averages on the Nelson Biology Test. The students are also scoring from ten to fifteen percentile points higher on the Nelson Biology Test than did the students at West Lafayette High School before the *Systems Approach to Biology* was instituted. All students who complete the course earn a grade of C or better. If a student does not complete the quizzes on each module, an incomplete (I) is recorded on his record until he demonstrates basic mastery of each of the modules. Sometimes, a student may not complete the course until the following year. The percentages of students receiving the grades of A, B, and C varies from year to year. Approximately sixty-eight percent of the students earn an A or B at the end of the course; another thirty-one percent or so earn a C; and about one percent receive an Incomplete. To date, all of the students who received an I later completed the requirements for an A, B or C.

[2]Curtis L. Smiley, Kenneth H. Bush, and David McGaw, "Student Involvement in the 'Systems Approach to Biology,'" *The American Biology Teacher*, vol. 35, no. 3 (March, 1973).

UNIT SIX--ENERGY; WHAT A BLAST

ABSTRACT

Consider how much work it takes to keep your room at home in order. It requires a bit of energy (probably more than you are willing to spend). Consider the energy required to keep a grocery store "in order" and functioning; that's a great deal more energy than that needed to keep your room in order. Do you realize that your body is composed of many more individual cells than the number of cans that grocery store has on its shelves, and that these cells must also be kept "in order?"

Some cells are destroyed by disease, some abraded or sloughed off, some are called upon to secrete substances, some to contract or move, some to conduct impulses and some to convert and store specific substances. Energy is required to repair or replace these cells and to carry out their cellular functions. Where does the energy come from? That's easy, from the food we eat. Where does the food come from? That's easy, from plants and animals. What is the ultimate source of the energy we require? THE SUN.

This unit is about the energy of the sun and its conversion to chemical energy, the form of energy that plants and animals can use. It concerns both the production and utilization of energy and terminates with a module concerning that very exciting question "how did life begin."

The unit consists of five modules, three inquiries, and two values.

From K. L. Bush, David H. McGaw, and Curtis L. Smiley, *Systems Approach to Biology Energy Study Guide,* ed. Robert N. Hurst. West Lafayette, Indiana: Diversified Educational Enterprises Incorporated, 1971, pp. 157, 158, 168, 170, 171, 179 and 181.

UNIT SIX--ENERGY--CHECK LIST

	Date Due	Date Completed	A/B Points
Module E-1 The Nature of Light and Pigments			
Module E-2 Chloroplasts and Mitochondria			
Module E-3 Photosynthesis			
Module E-4 Respiration			
Module E-5 The Heterotroph Hypothesis			
Oral Quiz E-1 and E-2			
Written Quiz E-1 and E-2			
Oral Quiz E-3			
Written Quiz E-3			
Oral Quiz E-4 and E-5			
Written Quiz E-4 and E-5			
Credit may be received for any three of these inquiries @ 10ea.			30
Inquiry #1 A Chromatogram of Food Coloring			
Inquiry #2 Photosynthesis			
Inquiry #3 Respiration			
Inquiry #4 Student-Designed Inquiry			
Value One-Thermal Pollution			10
Value Two-Alcohol Problems			10
Performance Instructor #1			10
Performance Instructor #2			10
Performance Instructor #3			10
A/B Test			40
		TOTAL POINTS	120

A =   points

B =   points

Module E-3 PHOTOSYNTHESIS--HOW IS SUGAR SYNTHESIZED?

RATIONALE

Water is split (photolysis) in the light reaction, and sugars are synthesized in the dark reaction. The dark reaction is temperature sensitive and photosythesis in general is dependent on many other environmental factors. This module will explore the relationships of these environmental factors to the process and rate of photosynthesis. Hopefully, the student will appreciate more fully the activity of the green plants after completing this module.

PERFORMANCE OBJECTIVES

After completing this module, the student should be able to:

1. Describe and recognize the events which take place during the dark reaction.
2. Describe or recognize an experiment which tests the hypothesis "light is necessary for photosynthesis."
3. Draw a graph showing the effect of light intensity on the rate of photosynthesis.
4. Relate the role of light to the conversion of sugar to starch.
5. Describe or recognize an experiment which tests the hypothesis "CO_2 is necessary for photosynthesis."
6. Describe or recognize an experiment which tests the hypothesis "chlorophyll is necessary for photosynthesis."

ADDITIONAL OBJECTIVES

READING OPTIONS

Module E-3 PHOTOSYNTHESIS--HOW IS SUGAR SYNTHESIZED?

PO 1 What general events occur during the dark reaction?

PO 2 Is light necessary for photosynthesis?

    1. describe the starch test.

    2. diagram the experiment.

    3. conclusions.

PO 3 The effect of light intensity on the rate of photosynthesis.

    1. diagram the experiment.

    2. conclusions

PO 4 Light and sugar conversion.

    1. diagram the experiment.

    2. conclusions.

PO 5   Is CO_2 neccessary for photosynthesis?

    1. diagram the experiment.

    2. conclusions.

PO 6   Is chlorophyll necessary for photosynthesis?

    1. diagram the experiment.

    2. diagram the leaves.

    3. conclusion.

INQUIRY #2   PHOTOSYNTHESIS

PERFORMANCE OBJECTIVES - After completing this inquiry, the student
should be able to:
1. List at least 15 variables for the photosynthetic process.
2. Write an inference for each variable.
3. Complete experimentation to "prove" at least two of the
    inferences.

MATERIALS -
     test tubes
     Elodea plants
     lights
     pin
     beakers
     ice

PROCEDURE - The experimental setups diagramed below yielded the
following results: Setup #1 produced 20 bubbles per minute (an
indirect measure of photosynthesis). Setup #2 produced 5 bubbles
of gas per minute. Remember you can only experiment with one
set of variables at a time.

DEFINITIONS -
1. Variable: A variable is some part of an experiment which is
    different in setup #1 and setup #2.
2. Inference: An inference is a statement relating the variable
    to the results.
         example of an inference: Elodea will form more gas
         bubbles in a given period of time (indicating the
         rate of photosynthesis) in a CO_2-rich environment.

| Setup #1 | Setup #2 |
| 20 bubbles per minute | 5 bubbles per minute |

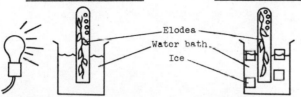

Close to the light source   Farther from the light source
Sodium bicarbonate added (a source of CO_2)

VALUE ONE--THERMAL POLLUTION

It has long been advocated that using nuclear energy as a source of power would be the most efficient way to produce electricity. However, we find that wherever nuclear power plants are now in operation, the water necessary to cool the atomic piles is warming up the streams into which it flows. This in turn is changing the environmental conditions of the streams. Plants and animals which once inhabited the streams can no longer survive. State your belief whether we should continue to install more nuclear plants and support your statement.

VALUE TWO--ALCOHOL

Drunkedness and highway accidents are highly related. If a person consumes three drinks containing an ounce of alcohol each in a short period of time, how long should he wait before he drives?

Curt Smiley, one of the instructors, has found that students of higher ability normally require minimal help from an instructor, while students of lower ability normally require more help from the instructor. The modular approach permits the instructors to spend more time with the students of lower ability. Instruction becomes less teacher-centered and more student-centered. He also found that students of higher ability proceed more quickly through the course than students of lower ability.[3]

Excerpts from the unit on energy are reproduced on pages 102-108. Each unit is printed and packaged separately to facilitate flexibility. The abstract for this unit is presented on page 102. The unit checklist (see page 103) indicates the five modules which make up the unit and provides a place for the student to record mastery of both the oral and written quizes on each module, the inquiries, the values and performance instruction, along with the A/B test score. The checklist records the student's completion of each module as well as his bonus points earned. The study guide for Module 3 from this unit is reproduced on pages 104-106. One of the inquiries is shown on page 107, and the two values are described in an excerpt from the unit on page 108. The *Systems Approach to Biology* is just one example of the use of modular instruction.

USE OF MODULES FOR TOTAL HIGH SCHOOL CURRICULUM

At Leo High School near Fort Wayne, Indiana (grades 7–12 with over 700 students), teacher-made modules have been designed to be used independently by individual students for self-paced learning. Each module or "learning package" as they are called at Leo, focuses on one major idea and includes specific objectives which provide the basis for individual study. In order to accommodate each student's unique learning style, alternative materials and activities for achieving each objective are suggested to the student in the module. Provision is made for student use of a wide variety of commercially and locally produced media, such as selections from textbooks, pamphlets, magazines, programmed materials, filmstrips, film loops, 35mm slides, audiotapes and phonograph records. The variety of possible activities includes model building, experiments, acting/role playing, small group discussions, field studies and interviews. The faculty at Leo has found that the greater the diversity of material, media and methods of instruction in the module, the greater the utility of the module.

Although the modular package provides structure for learning experiences,

---

[3]Curtis L. Smiley, "A Comparative Study of Compulsory vs. Non-Compulsory Attendance in Secondary Biology Using the *Systems Approach to Biology* Program as the Method of Teaching" (Unpublished doctoral dissertation, Purdue University, May 1973).

decisions inherent in the use of the modules encourage the development of self-initiative and self-direction on the part of the student. Even greater self-initiating and self-directing experiences are made available to each student by including "quests" for enrichment study. Problem statements for quest activities are included with each module to stimulate the student to define a problem for quest study, carry out his research and state some valid conclusions for the problem which he has chosen.

In order to individualize the curriculum, the Leo faculty adapted the organizational and philosophical strategy provided by J. Lloyd Trump in the Model Schools Program.[4] The faculty divided the Leo High School curriculum into eight subject-matter areas.

Language Arts
Social Studies
Foreign Language
Fine Arts
Health Fitness and Recreation
Practical Arts
Math
Science

Within the curriculum, concepts were broken into three categories.

Essential—all students should learn these
Desirable—for students with average ability
Enriching—for students with high ability

Once this task was completed, the monumental task of preparing the learning packages began.

Let's examine a learning package in the language arts area entitled *English Poetry Since 1900*, designed by Carolyn Platt, a teacher at Leo High School. The major idea, components and objectives for this learning package are reproduced on page 112. Note that each of the sheets is coded in the lower left-hand corner. The "LA" identifies it as a part of the language arts area. The "III" refers to level three which means that it is normally intended for high school juniors and seniors. Level I is seventh and eighth grade; and level II learning packages are intended for freshmen and sophomores. "LP 675" is the number of this particular package. Adjunct materials and tests for this package are coded with the same number.

The learning package on *English Poetry Since 1900* is composed of two lessons and is designed for approximately two weeks of individual study. It

[4] J. Lloyd Trump and Delmas F. Miller, *Secondary School Curriculum Improvement* (Boston: Allyn and Bacon, 2nd ed. 1973).

requires about six to eight student-hours to complete. The first lesson is shown on page 112. Note particularly the instruction and the suggested learning activities. The activities are keyed to a textbook which is available in the resource center. The second lesson is presented on pages 113 and 114. The objective allows each student to present his report in a variety of formats: written, orally on an audiotape or directly to the teacher. The learning activities also provide alternatives: reading poetry or listening to poetry on phonograph records. After the student has completed the report in lesson two and has finished any of the optional activities, he is ready to take the posttest. In order to check himself to see if he is ready to take the posttest, a parallel self-test is provided in the learning package (see pages 114 and 115). The answers to the self-test are also provided in the learning package.

As in some of the other modular programs described earlier, quest activities are available for the students who wish to pursue the topic in greater depth. Five possible quest activities for Mrs. Platt's learning package on *English Poetry Since 1900* are shown on page 115.

After the modules were completed, the materials were assigned to one of the eight resource centers—one for each area of the curriculum. All materials referred to in a particular module are stored in the resource center in which the module is housed. There is only one traditional classroom in the school. It is set up for those students who aren't quite ready to assume the responsibility for their educational careers.

At Leo High School, each student has his own individual and carefully supervised schedule. His learning activities are divided into large group presentations, small group discussions and a large block of time for independent study which may be spent in a lab, a resource center or in the instructional materials center. Lounge visitation privileges and student activities are also a part of a student's schedule.

The large group presentation is entirely motivational and deals with a general topic. There is no attempt to teach a specific concept. The presentation may be done live by a teacher or guest speaker or through media such as film or videotape. Members of a curricular area team may take turns preparing for these presentations or may select one teacher who specializes in large group presentations.

The small group discussions are designed to use and reinforce the knowledge pupils gain from large groups and in independent study. They help the students crystallize values and form attitudes. These discussions allow pupils to learn to discuss controversial matters, to communicate effectively, to listen to and respect the opinions of others and to deal with people whose backgrounds and interests differ from their own. Topics for discussion are chosen by the students or the teacher. The teacher is present but usually does not enter the discussion except to serve as a "clarifier."

Modern Poetry

Major Idea

Today's expressions of disillusionment and discontent with society are an echo of the same ideas we find in English poetry written during and after World War I.

Components

1. The study of given poems by different authors brings the experiences of the 1900's into focus as part of one's literary background.
2. An analytical study of a theme or an individual poet increases one's understanding of how Englishmen interpreted life in the 1900's.

Objectives

1. Given titles of required poems, identify their authors.
2. Given significant lines from required poems, give the title of the poem and briefly interpret them in writing, relating them to the prevailing ideas of the times or the poet.
3. Report your depth study, in writing or orally.

LA III   LP 675

Modern Poetry Lesson I

Main Idea

The study of given poems by different authors brings the experiences of the 1900's into focus as part of one's literary background.

Objectives

1. Given titles of required poems, identify their authors.
2. Given significant lines from required poems, give the title of the poem and briefly interpret them in writing, relating them to the prevailing ideas of the times or the poet.

Instructions

Do activities #1 and #2. The other is helpful but is not required.

Learning Activities

1. Read "Poetry," p. 617-619, in *England in Literature* in the resource center. Note the main characteristics of the poetry and the important figures of this period.
2. Study these selected poems in *England in Literature*. They are some of the most familiar of modern English poems. What attitudes of the 1900's do they present?

      The Lake Isle of Innisfree (Yeats)   p. 620

Developed and designed by Carolyn Platt, Learning Package 675 on *Modern English Poetry*, pp. 1, 2, 4, 5, 6, and 8.

In Waste Places (Stephens)   p. 625
Sea-Fever (Masefield)   p. 630
The Barrel-Organ (Noyes)   p. 632
The Soldier (Brooks)   p. 636
The Dead (Brooks)   p. 636
Futility (Owen)   p. 637
The Hollow Men (Eliot)   p. 641
I Think Continually of Those (Spender)   p. 652
Do Not Go Gentle into that Good Night (Thomas)   p. 656
The Strings' Excitement (Auden) included at the end
    of this lesson.

3. Find the given information about the authors and the questions to help
   you interpret and understand the poems listed in activity #2.

LA III LP 675

Modern Poetry Lesson II

Main Idea

An analytical study of a theme or an individual poet increases one's
understanding of how Englishmen interpreted life in the 1900's.

Objective

Report your depth study. The report may be written or oral (on a tape or
directly to the teacher, Mrs. Platt). Turn in your written report just before
taking the post-test. Do your oral report before taking the post-test (the
teacher will verify that you've given the report).

Instructions

Do activities #1 and #2. The others are helpful but not required.

Learning Activities

1. Study an aspect of modern English poetry. Use these guidelines: (a) Use
   a minimum of six poems, (b) Analyze the poems by their themes,
   imagery, symbols—whatever fits with the way you've chosen to study
   them, (c) Relate an author's poetry to his experiences and outlook on
   life, (d) Report by giving specific examples from the poetry or other
   references, (3) As reference materials, use books or magazines in the
   resource center and the IMC, (f) Report on your study. If written, it
   should be two pages.

2. Choose from these suggestions for your analytical study, or choose
   your own subject:

   Study of one modern English poet
   Comparison of two modern English poets
   Disillusionment with World War I
   Use of isolated imagery and allusions
   Disillusionment with old beliefs and traditions
   Use of newly created symbols

Emphasis upon emotion and lyricism (during 1930's)

Comparison of specific poems of today with poems on same theme from earlier 1900's.

3. Read about modern English poetry in books which give surveys of English literature.

4. Listen to some modern English poetry read on records in the resource center.

>PR En. 6-6A Many Voices: Adventures in English Literature (Eliot and Thomas)
>
>PR En. 82 Alec Guinness Reads Spiritual and Religious Poetry and Prose (Sitwell, Eliot, Belloc and Betjeman)
>
>PR En. 40-41 Dylan Thomas
>
>PR En. 49 Caedmon Treasury of Modern Poets Reading (Eliot, Thomas, Sitwell and Auden)
>
>PR En. 90 Understanding and Appreciation of Poetry (Masefield, Yeats and Noyes)
>
>PR En. 45 John Masefield
>
>PR En. 92 A Boy Growing Up, Part I (Thomas)
>
>PR En. 93 A Boy Growing Up, Part II (Thomas)

5. Read the materials at the end of this package, titled "Guided Analysis of a Poem" and "Essay Analysis of a Poem." These examples of poetry analysis may give you some ideas to use in your own analysis for this lesson.

LA III   LP 675

Modern Poetry

Self-test

I. Match the poem titles with the authors. One author is used twice.

1.	The Soldier	a.	Eliot
2.	Do Not Go Gentle into that Good Night	b.	Masefield
3.	Sea-Fever	c.	Owen
4.	In Waste Places	d.	Brooke
5.	I Think Continually of Those	e.	Spender
6.	The Dead	f.	Auden
7.	The Lake Isle of Innisfree	g.	Thomas
8.	The Barrel-Organ	h.	Noyes
9.	The Hollow Men	i.	Yeats
10.	Futility	j.	Stephens
11.	The Strings' Excitement		

II. The following lines are from some of the above poems. Give the title of the poem and write a brief interpretation of the given lines.

1. This is the way the world ends
   Not with a bang but a whimper.

2. They are crammed and jammed in buses
   and—they're each of them alone
   In the land where the dead dreams go.

3. If I should die, think only this of me:
   That there's some corner of a foreign field
   That is forever England. There shall be
   In that rich earth a richer dust concealed.

4. The names of those who in their lives fought for life
   Who wore at their hearts the fires center.
   Born of the sun they traveled a short while toward the sun,
   And left the vivid air signed with their honor.

LA III   LP 675

Modern Poetry

Quest

1. Read additional poems by any author which you particularly liked in this learning package.

2. Report on the English involvement and strategy in World War I.

3. Find out how England was affected by the Depression of 1929.

4. Do a study of English poetry which reflects the influence of the sea upon the Englishman's thinking.

5. Read writers of the Irish Renaissance, poets, dramatists and short story writers.

LA III   LP 675

Independent study time is spent either in the lab, the resource center or in the instructional materials center. The student's learning activities are specified in the learning packages. If a problem of "I don't understand" develops, the student asks the lab assistant or the resource center clerk for help. If these persons are unable to provide an answer, the student schedules a conference with the teacher who constructed the package or with someone who is a specialist in that field. Most teaching and learning takes place on a one-to-one basis.

Under the traditional semester system at most high schools, if a student fails two segments of the course during an eighteen week semester, he must repeat the entire semester. Furthermore, if a student fails just one portion of the semester, he is allowed to continue without ever being given the opportunity to learn that material which he failed to comprehend. Under the modular approach at Leo High School, if a student fails on a particular module, he repeats only that module and not the entire course or semester. A student is not allowed to move to a higher level module until he has learned the material that precedes it in the sequence.

At Leo High School, modular packages allow each student to pace himself.

Each package is multi-level, especially the beginning modules. The faster student moves rapidly through these beginning modules, doing only a few of the learning activities in order to meet the objectives, while the slower learner moves at his own pace, doing most or all of the learning activities and even repeating some, if necessary, until he has met the objectives. Thus, both groups of students are able to master the objectives. The students are not in competition with each other. Instead, both are trying to meet the objectives at their own rate.

Three of the most important aspects of the modular packages at Leo High School are behavioral objectives, alternative materials for achieving each objective and quest activities. The objectives tell the student and the teacher exactly what is expected of him. With alternative materials, the student is no longer limited to only the text but is allowed to utilize other forms of media which fit his individual learning style. Quests are an in-depth study of an area or topic which is found to be interesting to the student.

If the student does extremely well on the pretest, he may skip to the posttest and complete the requirement for the module. The questions which are missed on the pretest indicate which objectives the student needs to work toward and which of the learning activities will help him to achieve these objectives. Self-tests are also included to serve as a "self-diagnosis." The suggested learning activities are multi-level and varied. In many cases, the student does not have to do all of the activities to achieve the objectives. There are at least three different versions of the posttest. These are administered and graded by paraprofessionals in most cases. If the student does not pass the posttest, he will recycle through the material. He may not continue until he has meet the minimum requirements (or mastery level) for the module.

The traditionally designed school with individual classrooms for thirty students and one teacher does not provide the best facilities for the effective utilization of the modular approach. However, the Leo faculty has been able to make the necessary adjustments and has been very successful in the use of modular materials with their students. Teachers have specialized. No longer does the physics teacher have a general math class, a general science class and a girl's physical education class. Each teacher is assigned to one of the eight curriculum areas. Each teacher has twenty students whom he advises. Based upon information from the professional counselors, the student's records and the student's interests, the teacher-advisors help design a program of study which fits the individual student. In addition to working with students, the teacher spends time designing, developing and revising the modules. The teachers implement revisions with the addition of new information and adaptation of materials to approximately one-fifth of the modules each year. Teachers also need time to preview new materials for possible use with their modules. If necessary media cannot be purchased, the teachers meet with a media specialist who helps them design what is needed and then it is produced locally. It is also important that the teachers become familiar with new methods of instruction and keep up with new knowledge in their subject field.

The teachers are organized into subject area teams. The team evaluates the total effectiveness of its area of the curriculum, prepares motivational large group presentations and evaluates teaching techniques in each other's modules. Each teacher has office hours so that students having problems may meet with him for help. Also, the students who are interested in quest activities can meet with the teacher and the in-depth study is designed by the student and the teacher. Office hours are also used to meet with the teacher's advisees. In these private sessions, the teacher-advisor assesses the individual's progress, helps him determine his goals and motivates him to achieve his fullest potential.

Leo High School also employs about thirty paraprofessionals. The teacher aides supervise the halls, sell lunch tickets and handle attendance. The clerks handle typing, duplicating materials and operating the resource centers. The instructional assistants have special training and may be in a resource center but more often are in charge of the laboratories. An example would be an individual who has two years of college with a chemistry major and is assisting in the chemistry lab.

An academic student at Leo may select those modules in practical arts which he feels will benefit him as an adult. In fact, *all* students cover the essentials in all eight areas for a basic education. A student's daily schedule includes such things as:

Large Group Presentations—there is one presentation per area per week. The large group presentation is designed to motivate and create interest.

Small Group Discussions—there is one per area per week, and they reinforce ideas from the large group presentation, crystallize values, provide an opportunity for the formation of attitudes and teach respect for others' opinions. The students have time to discuss ideas, to communicate feelings and to relate in-school activities to the outside world.

Independent Study—a large portion of a student's time is spent in independent study. During independent study time, the student works on projects, quests and learning packages, such as the one described earlier.

If the student has problems, his first step is to ask the lab assistant or the resource center person. Frequently asked questions require only brief explanations of instructions or whether a pencil or a pen should be used. If, however, the student does have a problem with the content, he can consult one of the professional staff making his daily visits to the labs and resource centers or the student may make an appointment with the teacher for a help session. Even though the student has a definite schedule to follow, upon request the teacher-advisor may allow the student large blocks of study time per week in his area of interest if the student is doing well in the other areas. The modular approach allows continuous progress. The student could miss a week or more and still not really be behind since his progress is not subject to the progress of the class.

Another school using modules for its total curriculum is Nova High School in Fort Lauderdale, Florida. The staff of Nova High School has developed a modular approach to instruction using learning activity packages, usually referred to as LAPs. The Nova teachers are concerned about the students as individuals and have organized the instructional staff, the schedule, the facilities and the curricular materials to facilitate the individualization to instruction. A key component in the approach is the learning activity package or LAP. A LAP uses a variety of instructional media and provides each student with alternatives of how, what, when and where to learn the stated specific objectives. To illustrate, in a social studies LAP on "Man and His World in the Twentieth Century," there are required readings; the student views one of two commercially-available films, "People by the Billion" or "The Population Problem," and later uses a teacher-prepared videotape presentation entitled "People and Technology."

Some of the LAPs are designed for small group use. From an English LAP entitled "Hedonism," a set of instructions for small group discussion states:

> You will *listen* to various brief pieces of music which in turn will be *matched* with short pieces of poetry in the attempt to match mood, or style, or sensual appeal, or structure. The technique will be: *Playing and listening* to the music, briefly *matching* the poems, oral comments on the appropriateness of the results.[5]

ENRICHMENT

For students who are highly motivated to learn more about a topic, modules can be utilized to provide enrichment. Some teachers require students to complete certain basic modules and then select a given number of units from a pool of optional modules. In all subject-matter areas, there are an endless number of topics which some student might like to pursue in detail. For example, in social studies after having studied about South Africa, a module such as "South Africa—Apartheid"[6] by Jackie Wright, a graduate student in history at Purdue University, could be used as an enrichment activity. The module was designed for eighth and ninth grade students but could be adapted for grades four through twelve. The module can be used in a variety of formats. Part of the module is for individual use, and other parts can be used by a group

[5] Jan McNeil and James E. Smith, "The Multi's at Nova," *Educational Screen and Audiovisual Guide*, January, 1968.

[6] Apartheid is the official policy of political, social and economic discrimination and segregation enforced against non-whites in the Republic of South Africa.

South Africa—Apartheid
Jackie Wright
History Department
Purdue University

Objectives

1. Given a blank map, students should be able to diagram the population distribution of races in South Africa. Acceptable performance would be the inclusion of the following:

   a. Whites greatly outnumbered by blacks.
   b. Blacks and whites segregated in the cities.
   c. Blacks confined to reservations.
   d. Small numbers of whites controlling farmland outside the reservations.

2. Students should be able to list three reasons why the whites keep the blacks on the reservations. Acceptable answers would include three of the following:

   a. Desire for land
   b. Belief in white supremacy
   c. Discovery of gold on natives' land
   d. Discovery of diamonds on natives' land
   e. Fear of unification of the tribes against the whites
   f. Facility in control of the blacks
   g. Fear of miscegenation

3. Students should be able to list some of the defenses and criticisms of apartheid. Acceptable performance would be a balance sheet with at least three of the following points on each side:

   PRO SIDE
   a. Blacks are "happy and contented."
   b. Blacks are able to determine own laws within reservations.
   c. Blacks keep their culture and traditions.
   d. Whites are of a "superior race."
   e. Blacks do not have the technology or knowledge of farm skills—the result is wasted and eroded land.

   CON SIDE
   a. Blacks greatly outnumber whites yet have no real voice in their government.
   b. Blacks and whites should have equal rights.
   c. Whites are squandering the mineral and land wealth while the majority of the blacks are poor.
   d. Whites were invaders—the blacks are the rightful owners.
   e. Whites own a disproportionate amount of land compared to their relative population in the country.

Designed and developed by Jackie Wright, Study Guide for *South Africa—Apartheid,* pp. 1-2.

4. Students should be able to describe why the blacks have not rebelled against the white minority. Acceptable description would include at least three reasons from among the following:

   a. Blacks are not unified.
   b. Whites have the weapons.
   c. Whites control the government.
   d. Whites control the port cities and markets.
   e. Blacks are poor and must expend most of their time and energy making a living.
   f. Blacks lack leadership and education.
   g. Blacks have been conditioned to obey and fear the whites because of past terrorism.
   h. The powerful white army and police force continually watch out for subversive groups and always imprison the leaders.

of four to six students. The objectives are reproduced on page 119. The module includes a simulation game to be played by a small group of students, filmstrips which can be viewed individually or in groups and an article from *Issues Today* entitled "Apartheid: Self-Determination or Racial Enslavement?" The purpose of the game is to introduce the students to apartheid and the controversy which surrounds it. The game also gives the students some historical background and an awareness of the sequential development of the conditions as they exist today. The filmstrips are distributed by the South African government and are very complimentary to the system of apartheid. Their basic premise is that the system is the surest way to insure racial self-determination and to continue South Africa on its way to wealth and progress. The filmstrips have been included to strike a balance between defenses and criticisms of apartheid. The developer felt that it was important that both viewpoints be expressed in the module. The article from *Issues Today* presents a case study on minority groups in South Africa. The article gives both sides of the issue. It raises deep social and moral questions concerning human rights. The questions serve as a take-off point for additional quest activities or discussions.

Initially, the game is used to allow the students to discover the details of apartheid in an interesting way that is more motivating than merely reading a description of apartheid. The game presents a view of a system stacked in favor of the whites and therefore presents a view toward apartheid as an unjust and oppressive system. The module next prescribes the filmstrips which present the positive side of the issue. Finally, the article provides a good summary of the key issues and opens the door for further investigation and discussion.

The module serves as an example of material which is most appropriately used as enrichment for students who wish to pursue an area or special topic in greater detail. The teacher would not have time in a traditional curriculum to present many detailed topics, such as apartheid; however, with a modular approach, the teacher can prepare a series of modules on specialized issues and allow the advanced students to select those which interest them.

REMEDIAL INSTRUCTION

At the other end of the continuum, remedial instruction can also be accomplished by using modules. Class size in typical high schools and colleges sometimes prohibits individual attention to students having difficulty; therefore, many times they cannot receive as much help from the teacher as they need. These students can use "tutorial" modules in lieu of a teacher's personal

---

Plotting Points
Jo Meyer
Beach Grove High School
Indianapolis, Indiana

Abstract

This is a minicourse on plotting points on a rectangular coordinate system. The basic concepts of the number line are reviewed. You will be introduced to a two-dimensional system through an activity using a map. The characteristics of the rectangular coordinate system are presented. You will view a film on plotting points and then plot several sets of points to produce pictures.

Prerequisites

You should already know how to construct a number line, how to represent points on the number line and have a sense of positive and negative.

Objectives

Upon completion of this minicourse, you should be able to:

1. Construct a rectangular or Cartesian coordinate axis and correctly label the x and y axes and units of the axes.
2. Identify the abscissa and ordinate of a coordinate pair and/or axis.
3. Number the quadrants of the coordinate system.
4. Label the coordinate axes showing in which quadrants x and y are positive and negative.
5. Plot points represented by coordinate pairs.

Developed and designed by Jo Meyer, Study Guide on *Plotting Points*, pp. 1-2.

attention. Sometimes, materials are designed for specific use as remedial instruction. However, it is possible to use self-instructional modules that were designed for regular instruction in an earlier grade as remedial material in a later grade.

For example, Jo Meyer, a high school math teacher, has developed a minicourse on plotting points on a rectangular or Cartesian coordinate system which could be used as regular instruction for ninth grade students or as remedial instruction in a later course for those students who have not mastered the objectives. The minicourse could be presented as part of a mathematics laboratory or could be used for plotting data in a science course. The minicourse covers the construction of a rectangular coordinate system and plotting points on this system. The abstract, prerequisites and objectives for this minicourse are shown on page 121. The learning activities in the minicourse which are controlled by an audiotape first ask the student to review the number line since this concept is prerequisite to rectangular coordinates which can be thought of as two number lines perpendicular to each other. The student is given the opportunity to review the construction of the number line and to locate points on the line. The activities are done in the student's study guide.

Next, the student locates places on a simple map with streets and avenues as a transition from a one-dimensional line to a two-dimensional system. The map provides a very concrete and realistic activity for the students. The rectangular coordinate system is then introduced as two perpendicular number lines used to locate points on a two-dimensional surface such as a map. The number lines are identified as the x- and y- axis. Mrs. Meyer produced a short film which graphically portrays the plotting of points. Seeing the point plot itself was found to be more effective than simply telling the student how to do it. The student can look at the film as many times as he desires.

After having viewed the film, the student actively becomes involved in plotting points using golf tees and a peg board. There is then a transition to plotting points on graph paper. The module contains a number of activity cards, each of which contains a set of points which, when connected in dot-to-dot format, produce a picture. Errors in locating points can be quickly seen as defects in the picture. Each student can do as many of the activity cards as he wants or until he has mastered the technique of plotting points. The "Plotting Points" module is an example of using individualized material for remedial assistance to students.

ESTABLISHING ENTRY BEHAVIOR

Modules can be used in the classroom to achieve a certain prerequisite level of competency or "entry behavior." For example, in a high school physics class, a module could be used to provide students with a prerequisite competency with power of ten notation, which is necessary to develop skill in quickly solving physics problems. At the onset, some of the students might be very proficient with power of ten manipulations; others could have been introduced to the technique but lost competency because they were not required to use their newly acquired skill; still others might never have been introduced to this very useful technique. The instructional module on power of ten notation eliminates the need to devote class time to the subject which, due to student diversity, would bore some and confuse others. The students could be asked to master the material in the module on their own. Those who know the technique could ignore the material; those who had previously learned the skill but were a little "rusty" could use the module as a review; and those who had never been exposed to power of ten notation could learn the necessary manipulations on their own. All students could be required to pass a criterion test demonstrating their mastery of power of ten manipulations.

ABSENTEE INSTRUCTION

Modules can be used to provide continuous learning experiences for students who miss specific instruction due to absenteeism. Modular instruction can be especially useful for students who are hospitalized or confined at home. Since many modules are portable, the student's study location—at home, in school or in a hospital—is irrelevant.

For instruction in the primary grades where the students are essentially nonreaders, audiotapes can be used to present verbal information. For a module on animals, audio recordings could reproduce the sounds of the animals. Scale models of the animals would also be an integral part of the module. Pictures with the names of the animals along with the models and audiotape could be put into a convenient package, such as a shoe box, to be sent home for the student to use while recovering from a physically-impairing accident or illness.

Joyce Andrew, a first grade teacher at Glen Acres School in Lafayette, Indiana, has developed a multi-media module on zoo animals. In this module, the students learn the names of common zoo animals. They also learn to identify the animals in pictures and to read the names of the animals. The objectives are listed on page 124. When the module is used in the classroom, a film entitled "The Zoo" is shown to give the children the feeling of visiting a zoo. The film shows a visit to the Brookfield Zoo. It includes many of the animals that are included in the objectives, particularly the larger animals.

To give the children practice in recognizing animals and their physical characteristics, slides are used for group instruction and photographs or color pictures are included for individual use. Word cards containing the names of the

Zoo Animals
Bonnie Joyce Andrew
Glen Acres Elementary School
Lafayette, Indiana

Performance Objectives

1. The student will name the following zoo animals when shown a picture of the animal. Acceptable performance will be naming the animal correctly ninety percent of the time.

elephant	alligator	porcupine
lion	snake	opossum
giraffe	seal	penguin
tiger	wolf	kangaroo
rhinoceros	brown bear	antelope
hippopotamus	polar bear	leopard
ostrich	zebra	peacock
chimpanzee	monkey	camel

2. The student will read the names of the above listed animals. Acceptable performance will be correctly reading the name ninety percent of the time.

3. The student will match a word card with an animal name to a picture of that animal. Acceptable performance will be correctly matching the word and the picture ninety percent of the time.

Designed and developed by Bonnie Joyce Andrew, Study Guide on *Zoo Animals*, p. 1.

zoo animals listed in objective one are used to help the children learn to read the names of the animals. These can be used in large groups, small groups or individually. Picture books can also be used to point out various animals and their identifying characteristics. The students who are better readers will be able to read some of the information about the animals independently. At school, the teacher can read the information for the students who cannot read, and at home the parent can read to the child.

View-Master stereo picture reels can be used separately or in conjunction with a teacher-made audiotape. A couple of reels are appropriate for this module— "Wild Animals of the World" and "Wild Animals of Africa." These have been found to be fun and highly motivating for the children as well as helpful for them in learning the names of the animals in spoken and written form.

To assist in matching the name with the picture of the animal, Mrs. Andrew prepared a series of puzzles with two parts, one half showing a picture of an animal and the other half containing the name of that animal. The puzzles were designed so that the name would interlock only with the proper picture.

As an enrichment activity, Mrs. Andrew also developed a game which she calls

"Catch Me If You Can." It requires two to four players. One takes the role of a monkey who escapes from his cage at the zoo, and the other players are the zoo keepers who try to catch the escaped monkey. The student who portrays the monkey begins by taking two turns to give him a headstart. He must follow the path from his cage to the zoo gate. The other players (zoo keepers) then follow. Each player has one throw of the dice per turn. Each player advances the number of spaces shown by the number on the dice. If he lands on a colored space, he must draw a card of that color and pronounce the name of the animal printed on the back of the card. The names on the cards are from objective one. If the player can pronounce the name correctly, he gets to remain on that space; if he cannot, he must return to his previous location. There are occasional spaces which give special instructions, such as "The lion roars, run ahead three spaces!" If the monkey follows the path and gets to the zoo gate first, he escapes and is considered the winner. If one of the zoo keepers gets to the gate first, he is credited with capturing the monkey and declared the winner. Actually, all the children are "winners" because they are learning one of the objectives in addition to practicing counting skills and benefiting from the socialization of playing a game with each other.

All of the activities in the *Zoo Animals* module, with the exception of the above game, could be sent home for students who must be absent.

CORRESPONDENCE COURSES

Is it possible for students to learn outside the hallowed walls of the school? In 1967, Dr. Frank Mercer,[7] chairman of the Department of Biological Sciences at Macquarie University in Sydney, Australia, was charged with the task of preparing an equivalent undergraduate program in biology leading to a B.S. degree for both internal (on campus) students and external (off campus) students. The external students who live many miles from the university study at home thirteen weeks during the term with only five or six days on the campus. Initially, Dr. Mercer developed a correspondence-type course in introductory biology with a syllabus and printed materials covering the weekly lectures. The laboratory periods were conducted during the few days when the external students could come to the campus. In contrast, the internal students had laboratory activities each week. Dr. Mercer found that experimental work designed to illustrate lecture material is most effective when the laboratory period closely follows the lecture.

[7] Heather Adamson and Frank Mercer, "The Impact of External Teaching on Traditional Approaches to the Teaching of Biology at Macquarie University," *The Australian University*, 8(November, 1970): 97-125.

During the next year (1968), the external students were supplied with audio-tutorial units (modules) to cover the descriptive part of the course together with a kit including a microscope and other supplies for doing the experimental work at home. The modules proved to be an immediate success since they allowed external students to do their practical work during the term rather than concentrating it during a few days in the middle of the semester. The result was an integration of the lecture and the laboratory.

In fact, the modular approach was so successful in allowing the external students to carry out the experimental and observational studies away from the campus that the following year (1969) kits were also issued to internal students. The use of the kits overcame some of the limitations imposed by the strict timetables of laboratory periods in the internal course. Most of the internal students indicated that they learned more from an experiment conducted at home than one done in the laboratory. The approach has not only proven successful with the introductory course, it is now used with both internal and external students at all levels.

For home study, modules can be checked out in suitcase or package form and taken to the library or dormitory. The potential which modules offer in breaking down the walls and extending education is only limited by the creativity and imagination of their users. In addition to correspondence-type instruction at home for students who are located many miles from the university, modules can be used for study clubs and even behind prison walls. Some people may want to learn to satisfy an interest or just for the sake of learning with no intention of getting a degree.

With the increasing costs of education and the cut-backs in available funds, cost-conscious educators are looking to alternative forms of instruction. It is becoming more economical to take the instruction to the student than to bring the student to instruction, particularly at the university level. A very high percentage of the student's cost for a college education today goes for transportation to and from the university and room and board while there. This factor is compounded even further if the student is forced to give up his job and source of income in order to go to the university. In addition, taking the instruction to the student eliminates some of the costs of maintaining the institutions themselves.

SUMMARY

The utilization of modules in education and training could be almost universal, that is, used in any instructional situation with any student. However, the author does not recommend that modules be used for all instruction with every student. Just as a variety of approaches is important with each module, so, too, a variety of instructional formats is important in a student's total curriculum.

Some possible applications of modules in regular instruction, enrichment, remedial instruction, establishing entry behavior, absentee instruction and correspondence courses have been described in detail in this chapter. The next chapter describes the implementation of modules including the role of the teacher, scheduling procedures, facilities, equipment and grading systems.

CHAPTER XII

Implementing
Modular Instruction

After reading and studying this chapter, you should be able to:

1. *Briefly describe the new role of the teacher when using modular materials. Your description should include at least three functions of the teacher using modules other than designing and developing the modules.*
2. *List five criteria which must be taken into consideration when scheduling modular materials.*
3. *Describe the type of facilities and equipment which you would need to implement modular instruction in your subject matter area.*
4. *Design a grading (or student evaluation) system which would be appropriate for your students.*

Before implementing modules, it is imperative that the teacher be thoroughly aware of the entire sequence of modules to be used in the course. The teacher can, as a result, provide more effective coordination of the modules with other instructional activities, such as lectures, group discussions and films.

The student's first exposure to modules is particularly important. Since attitudes toward new instructional strategies are usually formulated upon initial contact, students should experience immediate success with the materials. Teachers may deem it necessary to spend a few minutes explaining the modular approach to learning. The mechanics of using a module should be briefly explained. The operation of necessary equipment, such as tape recorders and film projectors, should be explained. It should be understood that each student will be working at his own pace—neither pushed faster than he can efficiently perform, nor held back if he works rapidly. Students should be encouraged to ask questions any time and especially if the material seems confusing. The teacher can spot weaknesses in the modules from such student comments.

ROLE OF THE TEACHER

The use of modular instruction in the classroom changes the role of the teacher from *a disseminator of knowledge* to *a director of learning.* Most present-day educators are practitioners of the "show-and-tell" method of presenting information. These teachers mistakenly assume that presentation of information is automatically followed by learning. Using audiotapes, films and tangible materials, modules provide access to real and simulated learning experiences. Thus, the teacher becomes an arranger of contingencies necessary for the students to achieve the desired objectives instead of a relater of information to be recorded, remembered and regurgitated (the 3 R's?).

When relieved of time-consuming explanations and routine presentations, the teacher has time to provide for the student's individual needs and to inspire further achievement through dynamic and creative education. Modular instruction does *not* eliminate teachers or make teaching easier, but it does add new and different dimensions to the functions of educators.

The teacher becomes a diagnostician. He should be able to detect a loss of interest or careless errors on the part of the students. The following observations should be made: Does each student have adequate prerequisite information? Does each student display evidence of comprehension? Does the student already have the desired terminal behavior?

The teacher may be a prescriber of instruction—outlining, if possible, a program of study which will meet the needs of each individual student. The goal should be for each student to *master* a maximum amount of material instead of having the class cover a required amount of text material for course credit. As Benjamin S. Bloom says, "Our basic task is to determine what we mean by mastery of the subject and to search for the methods and materials which will enable the largest proportion of our students to attain such mastery."[1]

When using modular materials, an important function of the teacher is to create and maintain interest. The teacher may also serve as a resource person for those students who have minor difficulties with the materials by serving as a tutor for those students and answering questions not discussed in the module.

[1] B. S. Bloom, J. T. Hastings, and G. F. Madaus, *Handbook on Formative and Summative Evaluation of Student Learning* (New York: McGraw-Hill, 1971), p. 52.

SCHEDULING

When scheduling modules, the teacher needs to take into consideration the complexity of the module and the ability of his students who will be learning via modular instruction. How long will it take the students to complete the module? After actually using a given module, this data will be available. When considering a new or unused module, one would have to estimate the time needed on the basis of validation data supplied by the producer/developer and an inspection of the module.

For most classes, the students who need the longest time will need as much as four times as long to complete the modules as the students who master it most quickly. Therefore, activities for those students who finish the material early must be provided. In the past, teachers have often "rewarded" students who finish early by giving them additional work. Under this system, students learn very quickly not to finish early. Some teachers feel that students should be able to select the activities to be done after they complete a module. What to do with those who finish early is not a problem, but a unique opportunity for creative achievement. Those talented students with newly acquired competencies can be guided into additional and more challenging learning activities, such as quests.

Two types of scheduling patterns are possible with modular instruction. One is the completely modularized pattern in which most, if not all, of the instruction is provided in an individualized format. The student is allowed to work through various modules at his own rate and to take the appropriate criterion tests any time he desires. Another pattern, a more common one, is the partially modularized pattern in which a portion of the instruction is provided by modules. The other portion of the instruction is provided by conventional teaching methods. While studying modules, the student may distribute his time in any manner as long as he keeps within a given time limit. The student is expected to take the criterion test with other students at a fixed time. Under *no* circumstances should a student be assigned a minimum amount of material to be covered within a single class period. If the teacher uses the partially modularized pattern, students who do not finish the assignment should be encouraged to work on the module at a later time.

FACILITIES AND EQUIPMENT

When using modular instruction, no special facilities or equipment are required, except perhaps the necessary equipment to play audiotapes or to project slides if these materials are included in the learning unit. Since a variety of approaches and instructional strategies will be used, all furniture should be movable and easy to arrange, thereby allowing for multiple use of space—

individual study, small group discussion or large group presentations. The teacher may facilitate individualization of instruction and increase the opportunities for learning with modular materials by a mere re-grouping of tables and chairs.

It is *not* essential to have booths or carrels, although they are more conducive to concentration during independent study. The booths may range from cardboard dividers placed on conventional tables to commercially produced carrels equipped with hot and cold running water. Within this range, there are masonite booths which can be purchased or built locally to designated specifications. The purpose of the booth is to provide each student with a micro-environment in which to study independently. Other activities in the room will not detract or interfere with individual learning efforts within the confines of a study carrel or booth.

In addition to booths for independent study, a variety of work and study areas may be used for a modular program. For example, an area for small group discussions, a quiet reading area and a film viewing area may be within one classroom or in a number of different rooms. Within a single room or learning center, one corner may be arranged with chairs and a table for small group discussions and another area may be designed for independent study using booths or carrels. In each booth are the study materials and tangibles for the self-study modules. The materials may include audio tapes and/or slides. There may be a small library with reference materials in the learning center, or the students may go to the library or media center for reading.

The types of equipment which are usually used in a modular study program include audiotape recorders, slide projectors and movie projectors. Tape players may be used in a variety of classroom learning activities. It is up to the creative teacher to devise ways to reap the most benefits from audio recordings. Some may include: lectures by guest speakers, interviews with famous people, presenting information, vocabulary building, drill and practice, testing and evaluation, as well as student use for reports and presentations.

When selecting an audiotape player, one may choose from an inexpensive playback-only unit which is almost an expendable item that can be thrown away if it breaks down or needs extensive repair or a very expensive tape player/recorder which usually requires much less maintenance and provides more dependable service and higher fidelity. Which is better cassette or reel-to-reel machines? The trend is toward cassette machines for a number of reasons, including the fact that they are lightweight and portable in addition to being less expensive. The cassette tape also provides several advantages over reel-to-reel tapes, such as ease of storage, lower cost and the fact that the cassette tape can be removed from the machine at any time without rewinding. The latter advantage facilitates a student stopping a module in progress, removing the tape and then coming back to the material later to pick up where he stopped.

Often the teacher may be limited by the equipment available at the media center or already purchased by the school. It is usually more economical to use available equipment and to purchase additional equipment compatible with that on hand so that, in the case of breakdown, the machines can be easily interchanged and so that fewer parts need to be stocked for repairs and replacement. Talk with other teachers who have used a specific type and brand of equipment before making any large investment. Don't just listen to the salesman!

GRADING MODULAR INSTRUCTION

Educators have been using the normal curve to grade students for so long that their grading philosophy is tightly anchored to it. Some believe that a certain percentage of students must be below average even in the *best* of classes. Many teachers are convinced that only a minority of their students will be able to learn what they teach.

Benjamin Bloom in his discussion of mastery learning describes the role of the normal curve and its inappropriateness for education.

> There is nothing sacred about the normal curve. It is the distribution most appropriate to chance and random activity. Education is a purposeful activity and we seek to have the students learn what we have to teach. If we are effective in our instruction, the distribution of achievement should be very different from the normal curve. In fact, we may even insist that our educational efforts have been *unsuccessful* to the extent to which our distribution of achievement approximates the normal distribution.[2]

The students should be given the performance objectives and the standards of evaluation at the beginning of each module. The teacher should obtain or construct criterion tests which can be used to determine whether the student has mastered the unit. If the student has not met the criteria, the tests can be used to diagnose his problem area. Additional study in this area may be prescribed to help him master the unit. The teacher's diagnosis should be accompanied by a specific prescription of what the student should do to achieve mastery. The criterion tests also provide valuable feedback for the teacher since they may identify parts of the module that need modification or supplementation. After establishing the criterion behavior, the teacher and students should work together toward maximum student achievement. Modules should enable the majority of the students to attain these goals. If not, the module and the teacher have failed—not the students!

The students who achieve the criterion behavior should be given a passing grade; under some systems, this is just "P" or "pass"; in other systems, this mastery level may be an A or a C. Accurate and up-to-date progress charts

[2]*Ibid.*, p. 45.

should be maintained for each student so that he is aware of his academic standing throughout the course. The evaluation criteria should also be available so that the student can compare his progress with the teacher's expectations. Many times, it is possible to give criterion tests after each module and to require that each student demonstrate mastery at a prescribed level (say ninety percent) before advancing to the next material. Feedback on his performance should be provided the student as rapidly as possible. Computer scoring machines can facilitate this task.

From experience, teachers have discovered that students working toward a criterion or standard and not competing against each other are more willing to assist each other. Consequently, learning becomes a cooperative (not competitive) process in which the better students strengthen their own learning by helping others.

Summary

The characteristics and fundamentals of modular instruction, the process by which modules can be developed and tested, as well as some examples of modules in use from kindergarten to college have been discussed. The techniques for the utilization of modules presented in this chapter are just suggestions. Each teacher and school *must* adapt the modular approach to their own students, objectives/goals, staff and facilities. Remember, there is nothing magic in the use of modules. Just as any other teaching strategy, modules can be misused. Even though the focus of modular instruction is on the student, the key component in the success of such a program is the *teacher!*

Note to Readers from the Author

I would be most happy to attempt to answer any questions you might have about any of the material presented in this book. I will also try to elaborate on or provide additional information about any of the ideas or techniques presented. If you have questions or would like additional information, please write to me at the address below and I will answer you as quickly as possible.

I would also welcome any comments, suggestions or criticisms which you have about *Modular Instruction*.

James Russell
Department of Education
Purdue University
West Lafayette, Indiana 47907

References

Baker, R. L., & Schutz, R. E. *Instructional product development*. New York: Van Nostrand Reinhold, 1971.

Block, J. H. *Mastery learning*. New York: Holt, Rinehart and Winston, 1971.

Creager, J. G., & Murray, D. L. *The use of modules in college biology teaching.* Washington, D.C.: Commission on Undergraduate Education in the Biological Sciences, 1971.

Dell, H. F. *Individualizing instruction*. Palo Alto, Calif.: Science Research Associates, 1972.

Esbensen, T. *Working with individualized instruction*. Palo Alto, Calif.: Fearon, 1968.

Friesen, P. A. *Designing instruction*. Santa Monica, Calif.: Miller Publishing, 1973.

Gunselman, M. *What are we learning about learning centers?* Oklahoma City, Okla.: Eagle Media, 1971.

Johnson, R. B., & Johnson, S. R. *Assuring learning with self-instructional packages*. Reading, Mass.: Addison-Wesley, 1973.

Kapfer, P. G., & Ovard, G. F. *Preparing and using individualized learning packages*. Englewood Cliffs, N.J.: Educational Technology Publications, 1971.

Kemp, J. E. *Instructional design*. Belmont, Calif.: Fearon, 1971.

Mager, R. F. *Preparing instructional objectives*. Palo Alto, Calif.: Fearon, 1962.

Postlethwait, S. N., Novak, J., & Murray, H. T. *The audio-tutorial approach to learning.* Minneapolis: Burgess, 1972.

Weisgerber, R. A. *Developmental efforts in individualized learning.* Itasca, Ill.: Peacock Publishers, 1971.

Weisgerber, R. A. *Perspectives in individualized learning.* Itasca, Ill.: Peacock Publishers, 1971.

Index

ability to understand instruction, 23
absentee instruction, 123-125
achievement, 27, *see also* effectiveness and gain
active participation by students, 4, 20
activities flow chart, 98
alternative materials, 116
analysis of learner characteristics, 63-68
analyzing a learning task, 49
Andrew, Joyce, 123
annotated list of selection sources, 75
aptitude, 23
association, 18
attitude scale, biology, 88-89
audio materials, 19
  sources of, 76
audio-tutorial approach, 2
audio-visual equipment, 74

behavioral objectives. *See* objectives
biology attitude scale, 88-89
biology program at West Lafayette H. S., 96-109

Bloom, B. S., 22, 50, 130, 133
booths, use of, 132

carrels, use of, 132
Carroll, J. A., 23
checklist
  for evaluating modules, 36
  for evaluating objectives, 49
  use of, 34
completion questions, 58
construction of criterion items, 53-61
  completion, 58
  essay, 59
  general guidelines, 56
  matching, 57
  multiple-choice, 57
  performance-type, 59
  short answer, 59
  true-false, 56
conventional instruction
  compared with modular instruction, 25-29
  converted to modules, 35
correspondence courses, 125-126
criterion items
  constructed response, 60

construction of, 40, 53-61
criterion-referenced, 61
norm-referenced, 61
selected response, 60
use of, 40, 60
criterion-referenced evaluation, 61
criterion test. *See* criterion items
critical questions, 55

design of modules, overview, 39-43

educational objectives. *See* objectives
effectiveness, definition, 92
efficiency, definition, 92
English Poetry Since 1900, 110-115
enrichment modules, 118-121
entry behavior
    modules for establishing,
        122-123
    specification of, 41, 63-68
    statements of, 65-67
entry test
    definition, 67
    use of, 41
equipment, 131-133
essay questions, 59
evaluation of modules, 42, 87-94

facilities, 131-133
failure of students, 29
feasibility study, 32
feedback, 42
films, sources of, 75
flexibility of modules, 4, 29
freedom with modules, 4, 27

Gagné, R. M., 18, 70
gain score, 93
grading modular instruction, 133-134
group size, 15
guidelines for test item construction, 56

human interaction, 20

immediate reinforcement, 21
implementation of modules,
    129-134
independent study, 115, 117
individual differences
    concern for, 1, 14

accommodating, 15
individualized instruction
    definition, 1
    with modules, 3, 26
inquiry activities, 96
inspection of modules, 34
instruction, sequencing of, 41,
    69-71
instructional objectives. *See* objectives
instructor's time, best use of, 100
interaction among students, 5

James, W., 18

LAP, 118
learner characteristics
    analysis of, 41, 63-68
    general, 64
    sample, 64
Learning Activity Package, 118
learning experiences, 25
learning hierarchy, 70-71
Leo High School modular program,
    109-118

Macquarie University, 125
Mager, R. F., 16, 18, 46, 47
mastery evaluation strategy, 22, 28,
    101
matching questions, 57
mean modified gain score, 93
media
    categories of, 19, 71
    selection of, 41, 71-77
    sources of, 75-76
    utilizing a variety of, 19, 26
Media Preference Hierarchy, 73
Mercer, Frank, 125
Mimicry minicourse, 5-12
minicourses. *See also* modules
    examples, 5-12
    Mimicry, 5-12
    implementation of, 2
Minicourse Evaluation Form, 90-91
Model Schools Program, 110
modified gain score, 93
modular instruction. *See also*
    modules
    characteristics of, 13
    compared with con-

ventional instruction, 25-29
fundamentals of, 13
modules
    absentee instruction, 123-125
    in correspondence courses,
        125-126
    definition of, 3, 12
    design of, 39-43
    enrichment use, 118-121
    entry behavior, 122-123
    evaluation of, 42, 89-94
    evaluation form, 90-91
    example, 5-12
    implementation, 129-134
    Mimicry, 5-12
    rationale for, 3
    remedial use, 121-122
    scheduling of, 131
    selection of, 31-37
    student tryout of, 79-85
    for total high school cur-
        riculum, 109-118
    utilization of, 95-127
multiple-choice questions, 57
multi-sensory learning, 8

normal curve, 22, 133
norm-referenced evaluation, 61
Nova High School, 118

objectives
    acceptable performance, 48
    advantages of, 16
    characteristics of, 16
    checklist for evaluating, 49
    components of, 46
    examples of, 46, 104, 112,
        119, 121, 124
    performance conditions, 47
    performance term, 46
    purposes of, 45
    research on, 16
    specification of, 40, 45-52
    statement of, 15
    use of, 25, 100

parallel test items, 54
paraprofessionals, use of, 117
participation
    active, 4
    by students, 4, 20, 26

performance instruction, 97, 99
performance objectives. *See* objectives
performance questions, 59
perseverance, 23
Platt, Carolyn, 110
portability, 28
Postlethwait, S. N., 2, 18, 20, 25
*Preparing Objectives for Programmed
    Instruction,* 16
printed materials, 19
process of selection, 33
programmed instruction
    characteristics of, 2
    using reinforcers, 22
projected materials, 19

quality of instruction, 23
quests, 110, 116

rate of learning, 26
real materials, 20
regular instruction, use of modules
    in, 96-109
reinforcement, 21, 27
relevant test items, 55
remedial instruction, 121-122
revisions, 29
role of teacher, 5, 25, 130
Rothkopf, E. Z., 35
Russell, J. D., 25

scheduling modules, 131
selection
    of materials, 25
    of media, 41, 71-77
    of modules, 31-37
    process of, 33
selection sources, annotated list
    of, 75
self-contained package, 14
self-instructional package, 14
sequencing
    of instruction, 18, 41, 69-71
    techniques for, 70
short-answer questions, 59
Skinner, B. F., 2, 21
small group discussions, 117
Smiley, B. L., 109
specification of entry behavior,
    63-68
strategies for learning, 26

structure of knowledge, 18
student
    demonstrations, 55
    failure, 29
    interaction, 5
    products, 55
    time, best use of, 100
student tryout, 42, 79-85
    evaluation sheet, 81
    with large group, 85
    of self-instructional modules,
        83-84
    with small group, 85
study guide, sample of, 102-108
Sub-objectives, 50
Systems Approach to Biology, 97-109

tangibles, 20
task analysis, 49
taxonomy of cognitive objectives, 50

teacher's role with modules, 5
terminal behavior, specification of,
    40
test items, construction from ob-
    jectives, 16. *See also* criterion
    items
testing procedures, 28
time allowed for learning, 24, 27
true-false questions, 56
Trump, J. Lloyd, 110
tryout of modules, 42, 79-85

utilization of modules, 95-127

value training, 96
visuals, 19

West Lafayette H. S. biology pro-
    gram 96-109
Wright, Jackie, 118